D0839157

DIVING & SNORKELING
Florida Keys

Bill Harrigan

lonely planet

MELBOURNE | LONDON | OAKLAND

Florida Keys

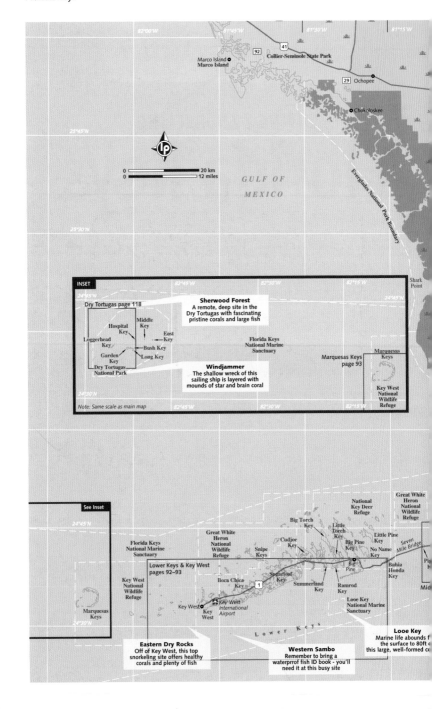

GULF OF MEXICO

Marco Island
Marco Island

Collier-Seminole State Park

Ochopee

Chokoloskee

Everglades National Park Boundary

Shark Point

0 — 20 km
0 — 12 miles

INSET

Dry Tortugas page 118

Middle Key
Hospital Key
East Key
Loggerhead Key
Bush Key
Garden Key
Long Key
Dry Tortugas National Park

Sherwood Forest
A remote, deep site in the Dry Tortugas with fascinating pristine corals and large fish

Florida Keys National Marine Sanctuary

Marquesas Keys page 93

Marquesas Keys

Windjammer
The shallow wreck of this sailing ship is layered with mounds of star and brain coral

Key West National Wildlife Refuge

Note: Same scale as main map

See Inset

National Key Deer Refuge

Great White Heron National Wildlife Refuge

Big Torch Key
Little Torch Key
Little Pine Key
Cudjoe Key
Big Pine Key
No Name Key
Seven Mile Bridge

Florida Keys National Marine Sanctuary

Great White Heron National Wildlife Refuge

Snipe Keys

Big Pine Key

Bahia Honda Key

Lower Keys & Key West pages 92–93

Boca Chica Key

Sugarloaf Key

Summerland Key

Ramrod Key

Looe Key National Marine Sanctuary

Mid

Key West National Wildlife Refuge

Key West
Key West International Airport
Key West

Marquesas Keys

L o w e r   K e y s

Looe Key
Marine life abounds f the surface to 80ft this large, well-formed c

Eastern Dry Rocks
Off of Key West, this top snorkeling site offers healthy corals and plenty of fish

Western Sambo
Remember to bring a waterprrof fish ID book - you'll need it at this busy site

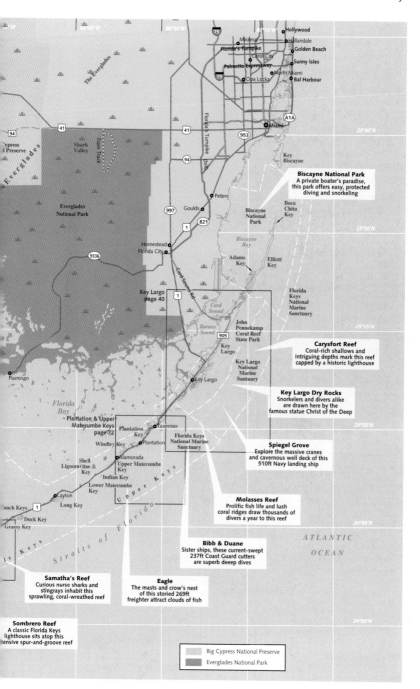

Biscayne National Park
A private boater's paradise, this park offers easy, protected diving and snorkeling

Carysfort Reef
Coral-rich shallows and intriguing depths mark this reef capped by a historic lighthouse

Key Largo Dry Rocks
Snorkelers and divers alike are drawn here by the famous statue Christ of the Deep

Spiegel Grove
Explore the massive cranes and cavernous well deck of this 510ft Navy landing ship

Molasses Reef
Prolific fish life and lush coral ridges draw thousands of divers a year to this reef

Bibb & Duane
Sister ships, these current-swept 237ft Coast Guard cutters are superb deeep dives

Samatha's Reef
Curious nurse sharks and stingrays inhabit this sprawling, coral-wreathed reef

Eagle
The masts and crow's nest of this storied 269ft freighter attract clouds of fish

Sombrero Reef
A classic Florida Keys lighthouse sits atop this extensive spur-and-groove reef

Key Largo
page 40

Plantation & Upper Matecumbe Keys
page 72

Big Cypress National Preserve

Everglades National Park

Diving & Snorkeling Florida Keys
4th edition – September 2006

Published by
Lonely Planet Publications Pty Ltd
ABN 36 005 607 983
90 Maribyrnong St, Footscray,
Victoria, 3011, Australia
www.lonelyplanet.com

Lonely Planet Offices
Australia Locked Bag 1, Footscray, Victoria, 3011
Phone 03 8379 8000 Fax 03 8379 8111
Email talk2us@lonelyplanet.com.au

USA 150 Linden St, Oakland, CA 94607
Phone 510 893 8555 Toll free 800 275 8555 Fax 510 893 8572
Email info@lonelyplanet.com

UK 72-82 Rosebery Ave London EC1R 4RW
Phone 020 7841 9000 Fax 020 7841 9001
Email go@lonelyplanet.co.uk

Author Bill Harrigan
Publisher Roz Hopkins
Publishing Manager Chris Rennie
Commissioning Editor Ben Handicott
Design Manager Brendan Dempsey
Mapping Development Paul Piaia
Project Management Annelies Mertens
Production Pepper Publishing (Aust) Pty Ltd
Print Production Manager Graham Imeson

Printed by C&C Offset Printing Co Ltd, China
Photographs Bill Harrigan (unless otherwise noted)

ISBN 1741040485

With Many Thanks to
Jennifer Bilos, Jo Vraca, Alison Lyall, Carol Chandler, Amy Carroll,
Angus Fleetwood, Tom Calderwood, Sayher Heffernan

Contents

Author

BILL HARRIGAN

Bill Harrigan graduated from Yale University in 1972 with a bachelor's degree in marine biology and later earned a master's degree in marine area management from the University of Rhode Island. During his career as a commissioned officer in the National Oceanic and Atmospheric Administration (NOAA), Bill served on research vessels in the Pacific and Alaska, and directed NOAA's Helicopter Operations Group in support of environmental research. He managed the Key Largo National Marine Sanctuary from 1984 to 1987 and directed the US National Marine Sanctuary and National Estuarine Research Reserve Programs in Washington, DC. His last assignment as a NOAA Corps officer was in Australia, where Bill directed the Planning and Management Section of the Great Barrier Reef Marine Park Authority. After retiring from the NOAA Corps in 1993, Bill became a field editor for *Skin Diver* and *Sport Diver* magazines, writing and photographing more than 300 dive travel articles. Bill also consults internationally on marine park management and teaches underwater photography.

FROM THE AUTHOR

Many people helped with the writing and photography in this book and I'm grateful to all of them. In particular I'd like to thank my wife Kathleen, Stephen Frink, Liz Johnson, Spencer Slate, Dave and Marie Harrigan, the entire Bors family, Joe Clark and Doc Schweinler, Joe Angelelli, Louie Chrispino, Craig Nappier, Rob Bleser, Kenny Wheeler, Ginger Gibson, Rob Haff, Jeff Cleary, Scott Rodman, John and Judy Halas, Michael Gilchrist, Ben Wilson, Richard Watkins, Amy Slate, Terry and Lana Ernst, Bob and CeCe Holston, Kyle Smith, Megan Collins and Marc Hightower.

PHOTO NOTES

Bill Harrigan's primary underwater camera is a Canon EOS 1Ds digital SLR in a SeaCam housing. For some images in this book, Bill also used a Nikon F-100 camera in a SeaCam housing and a pair of Nikonos V cameras. Ikelite strobes are used for underwater lighting, including a pair of Substrobe 200s, a pair of DX-125s and an MX-50. For topside photography, Bill relies on the Canon 1Ds and a Canon 20D. Principle topside lenses include Canon's 24-70mm and 70-200mm zooms. Over-under images are captured with SeaCam's Super Dome and Canon's 15 or 20mm lenses.

Introduction

The Florida Keys have been one of the world's most popular dive destinations for decades, and one of the sport's most recognizable icons. If you asked people who have come in the past what word best described the diving here, the top five answers would most likely be; shallow, coral, wrecks, easy and fishy.

All those words certainly apply, but there is much more to diving in the Keys. It's true that many dives are in the 10 to 50ft (3 to15m) range, and the snorkeling is great on reefs that are even shallower. However, there are also some excellent dives as deep as 130ft (39m). The coral reefs are definitely the heart of the Keys, but the live coral cover is significantly lower than many Pacific reefs, and about on par with much of the Caribbean. Wrecks abound, from ancient to recent, and the accessibility is incredible. The diving *is* easy – *most* of the time. Some sites are subject to very strong currents, and when the wind kicks up, surface conditions can get boisterous. As for fishy, no qualifiers are needed; the Keys may be the 'fishiest' sport diving destination anywhere.

There are certainly more dive sites available in the Florida Keys than are described in this book. However, these sites include the most popular dives and encompass the whole range of available diving.

The bronze statue called 'Christ of the Deep' has greeted Key Largo snorkelers and divers since 1966

Divers on a 'six pack' dive boat, carrying a maximum of six divers, admire Molasses Reef's clear waters and tall coral ridges

Facts about the Florida Keys

The Florida Keys are water, sun, coral, fish and people, with just enough land on which to eat, sleep and drive. Every visitor experiences a different mix of those ingredients, depending on their own interests. Here are some interesting facts to keep in mind as you make your way along the dive destination billed as 'the islands you can drive to.'

- The Overseas Hwy is 126 miles long and includes 42 bridges. Tolls were collected on portions of the road until 1954.
- There are about 1700 islands in the Florida Keys, but only 32 have significant inhabitation. The largest island, Key Largo, is about 30 miles long. Big Pine Key has an area of 9.9 sq miles (25.6 sq km).
- *Key Largo* starring Humphrey Bogart, Edward G Robinson and Lauren Bacall was filmed in Key Largo at the Caribbean Club in 1948.
- The Keys are located near the 25° north line of latitude.

- Zane Grey joined the Long Key Fishing Club in 1911, and worked on many of his books while staying there.
- Key West is closer to the equator than any other point in the continental US, but it is still 1473 nautical miles (2728km) away.
- The highest point on Key West is Solares Hill, with an elevation of 16ft (4.9m).
- There are only four 'towns' in the Florida Keys: Key West, Marathon, Key Colony Beach and Islamorada. The remainder of the Keys, including Key Largo, are unincorporated parts of Monroe County.
- Monroe County covers 996.9 sq miles (2582 sq km) of land and 2740.2 sq miles (7097 sq km) of water.
- The Florida Keys are known for diving and fishing, not for wide sandy beaches. There are some nice beaches, though, including Harry Harris Park (MM92), Anne's Beach (MM73), Sombrero Beach (MM50), Bahia Honda State Park (MM37) and Smathers Beach (Key West). Some resorts also have small private beaches.

HISTORY

To the casual visitor, the Florida Keys might seem like a sleepy little chain of islands basking in the sun, but the residents have always been ready to try something new. At various times they've been fishermen, shrimpers, farmers, cigar makers, turtle wranglers, wreckers, smugglers, soldiers, traders, film makers, researchers and even vacationing presidents.

The story begins, as history usually does in America, with the Indians. When Ponce de León first 'discovered' the Keys and claimed them for Spain in 1513, the Calusa and Tequesta Indians were already here. In fact, evidence such as

The sailing vessel Western Union, one of Key West's many historic sites

pottery remains suggest that the Keys were inhabited as far back as 1000 BC.

With no gold and little fresh water, the islands remained largely forgotten for the next 2½ centuries. By the early 1700s, settlers from the Bahamas were trickling into the Keys, at least long enough to rustle wood from the hardwood hammocks or to catch turtles. A staple of their diet was the queen conch, and they took pride in calling themselves conchs (pronounced konk).

By the early 1800s, a trading route was growing between the east coast and the Mississippi River, with the Keys right in the middle. In 1821, John Simonton purchased Key West from Juan Pablo Salas of Spain for the princely sum of $2000. With a good deep-water port established, shipping expanded rapidly. Unfortunately, many vessels wound up aground on the shallow reefs. Between 1830 and 1840 alone, more than 300 ships hit reefs in the Florida Keys. Salvaging the ships and their cargo was the job of the 'wreckers', a wild and ag-gressive group often accused of luring ships onto the reefs by extinguishing or moving lights on the shore. The roof top decks and tall observation towers still seen in Key West trace their origin to the wreckers, who would maintain a constant watch for grounded ships.

To save the ships, a series of light-houses were constructed, beginning around 1850. Since the reefs are well offshore, sometimes as far as six miles, conventional lighthouses on the coast would not have worked. Instead, light-houses featuring an elegant and unique design – with an open framework and 'screwpile' legs – were built directly on top of the reefs. Many of those lights are still working today, including Carys-fort, Alligator and Sombrero. As naviga-tion improved, wrecking died out and was replaced by more peaceful pursuits such as harvesting sponges, raising pineapples and catching lobster. At one time nearly every fence in Key West was hung with drying sponges, and stories abound of people wading out to knee-

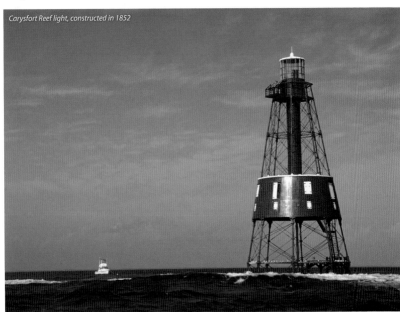

Carysfort Reef light, constructed in 1852

Observing the sunset is a daily celebration in the Florida Keys

deep water to catch lobster. Of course, synthetic sponges have largely replaced natural sponges, but lobstering is still a major fishery in the Keys, with about 3½ million pounds being caught in 2003.

Nothing has affected the history of the Florida Keys more than Henry Flagler's Florida East Coast Railroad. The project was started in 1905, and took seven years and $27 million to complete, earning it the nickname 'Flagler's Folly.' It was to operate for 23 years before finally showing a profit, but the railroad tied all the islands to the Florida mainland and created unparalleled access all the way to Key West. By 1935, about 50 million people had visited the Keys via the new rail line.

The Labor Day hurricane of that year spelled disaster for the railroad. The 18ft (5m) storm surge and 200mph (322km/h) winds killed 800 people and wiped out the railroad. The state of Florida bought the right-of-way and surviving bridges for $640,000 and began building a highway over the old railroad

Schooner Liberty in Key West harbor

bed. Today, that road is the dominant feature of the Keys, constantly moving people and goods along the islands. Without the road, the Keys would be a lazy backwater on a remote bayou.

The significance of the highway was publicly demonstrated in 1982 when the US Border Patrol set up a blockade at the entrance to the Keys in an ill-planned attempt to catch illegal immigrants from Cuba. Traffic quickly became hopelessly snarled, stranding residents and visitors in a hundred-mile gridlock. In mostly tongue-in-cheek

Fort Jefferson in the Dry Tortugas, constructed in the mid-1800s and later used as a prison

protest, the Keys formed a new nation, the Conch Republic, seceded for one minute, surrendered, then applied for foreign aid.

Government activities have always been part of the Florida Keys' history, and 19th century military installations like Fort Jefferson and Fort Zachary Taylor are still in existence. The Navy began its long-term relationship with the Keys during WWII, establishing ship bases and air stations that operate today. After the war, President Truman maintained a vacation home in Key West. During the Cold War years of the '50s and '60s, the Keys became part of the Nike missile system.

Fishing, diving and general tourism pay the rent these days in the Florida Keys, but remnants of the past are still visible along the Overseas Hwy. Watch for the forts, the old railroad bridges, the stacked lobster pots and the hurricane memorials, and pull off the road for a few minutes to immerse yourself in a bit of real Keys history.

GEOGRAPHY

The timeline that traces the geological formation of the Florida Keys and the coral reefs begins during the ice ages of the Pleistocene epoch. As the earth cooled, the polar caps expanded and sea levels receded worldwide. After that (but still about 150,000 years ago) a warm period, known as the Sangamon interglacial, slowly raised sea levels again, pushing them 25ft (7.6m) higher than today and putting all of what is now the Keys under water. This created a giant living coral reef stretching from the area where Miami would eventually be built all the way to the Dry Tortugas.

The limestone skeletons secreted by those ancient corals now comprise the bedrock of the Upper Keys. Scratch through the thin layer of dirt anywhere in Key Largo and you'll find a fossil reef beneath your feet. Better yet, if your dive boat passes through Adams Cut on the way to the reefs, check out the fossil coral exposed when the giant saws cut

The near shore waters of the Florida Keys are excellent for kayaking, especially in Florida Bay

the waterway. Star, brain and elkhorn fossils are on permanent display in this open-air museum of geology. The Windley Key Fossil Reef Geological State Park is another great place to see and touch the past. The park is open every day from 8:30am to dusk and you can find it at MM 85.5 on the bayside.

Things are a bit different in the Lower Keys. Oolitic rock – the limestone remains of calcareous algae from the ancient reefs – forms the foundations of the islands and surrounding reefs. Over time sea levels continued to rise and fall, leaving evidence of various distinct bands of coral reef. During the Holocene epoch, roughly 10,000 years ago, more global warming began. About 5000 years ago, water from melting ice caps spread over the low-lying landmass to mingle with the Gulf of Mexico and Atlantic Ocean. Florida Bay and the Everglades were formed, and what was once solid land in South Florida became more than 200 islands that now comprise the Florida Keys. The reefs we dive today are living on the top of calcium carbonate deposits left by coral polyps growing during the past 5000 or so years.

CLIMATE

Here's a four season climate report tailored for divers:

Spring (March to May) is a delight. Little rain, daytime temperatures in the 80s F (27° to 32°C), night-time in the 70s (21° to 27°C). Humidity will be low, at least for the Keys. Live in your shorts and T-shirts, with a jacket handy just in case. Water temperature will be around 80°F (27°C), warming up from the winter chill. A 3mm shorty works fine for most, a 3mm full suit might be better for thermally sensitive divers. Winds should be moderate, so wave conditions out on the reef should be tolerable to good.

Summer (June to August) is prime dive time. Afternoon thundershowers will bring some rain into the picture, but it comes down fast and then it's gone. Daytime temps will be in the 85° to 95°F (29° to 35°C) range, night-time temps will sag only to the high 70s or low 80s. Forget the jacket, unless it's a light rain jacket. Leave the wetsuit at home too, since the water temperature will be around 85°F (29°C). Dive in a bathing suit if you want, although many people wear Lycra suits, Polartecs or 1mm suits for protection against the sun and possible jellyfish. The rheostat is turned way down on the trade winds, so chances are good for flat calm or at least only mildly choppy water on the reefs. It's the start of the hurricane season, but not prime time.

Fall (September to November) is also great, unless there's actually a tropical storm in the area. Afternoon thundershowers are still a regular occurrence, but they're over quickly and the sun is back. Daytime temps are still high, but at night it's beginning to cool off more,

Place Names

Loggerhead Key in the Dry Tortugas

A map of the Florida Keys is dotted with colorful, and sometimes mysterious, names. Some are Bahamian in origin, some date back from the Calusa Indians and some are just plain head scratchers. El Radabob Key, for instance, in John Pennekamp Park, sounds like it might have been named by a Bedouin chief. Actually, El Radabob was originally Julia Island. It was generously donated to Pennekamp Park by the Crane family in the early 1960s and was renamed after four family members: Ellen, Radford, Dave and Bob. Some of the puzzling reef names are derived from ships that sunk on the spot, including the HMS *Carysford*, later corrupted to Carysfort; the HMS *Looe*, which grounded on Looe Key Reef in 1744; and the USS *Alligator*, which was lost on the reef named for it in 1822. **Pickles Reef** is not named for the ship that sunk there but for the ship's cargo of pickle barrels filled with cement mix.

Other Keys places are named after people long forgotten by most inhabitants. Rodriquez Key was named for Captain Melchor Rodriquez, a Spanish explorer from the later part of the 14th century. Knight's Key and Windley Key were both named after early settlers.

First impressions account for several place names. Spanish explorers observing Islamorada in the sunset gave it a name meaning 'purple island'. Sugarloaf Key and the Saddlebunch Keys reportedly take their names because they look like white loaves and saddles respectively. Key Largo of course is named for its large size, while Big Pine Key is named for both its trees and its girth.

Flagler railroad workers added their own place names to fill in the gaps. Lake Surprise turned out to be more difficult than expected to cross and Ohio Key was meant to remind the men of home. By the time the railroad reached the middle keys, most of the workers agreed that the whole project had turned into a real marathon, hence the name.

Snorkeling is family fun on reefs throughout the Florida Keys

perhaps into the low to mid 70s. Shorts and T-shirts are still the sartorial mainstay, but it's time to pack a light jacket or sweatshirt for the occasional dip in temp. The water is still warm, but it begins to fall slightly in November. A 3mm shorty will be about right for most, a 3mm full suit might be better for others. Those flat days of summer begin to dwindle as the trade winds start up again, but diving conditions are still good.

Winter (December to February) is when the snowbirds come, and the topside weather is truly wonderful. Daytime temps are in the 65° to 75°F (18° to 24°C) range, and nights are usually 60° to 70°F (16° to 21°C). Pack the usual shorts and T-shirts, but bring at least one pair of long pants and a sweater or jacket. Chances of rain are slim. The water temperature will drop to the 71° to 76°F (22° to 24°C) range, cold enough for a 3mm full wetsuit for most and a 5mm for the easily chilled, although many visitors still seem comfortable in the ubiquitous 3mm shorty. The trade winds reach their peak in the winter, although there are still calm days occasionally.

Bring a seasickness potion if you need it, because this is the season when the seas are roughest.

POPULATION & PEOPLE

The Florida Keys' first inhabitants passed this way several thousand years ago. They were migratory predecessors to the Calusa Indians, who left scant trace of themselves behind. European explorers arrived in the early 1500s, but mostly sailed on by for three centuries, leaving the Indians in relative peace. With the arrival of Bahamian and colonial settlers at the start of the 1800s, though, things changed. By 1830, the population had jumped to around 500 people. By midcentury the Indians, with the exception of the Seminoles, were driven out of Florida and the number of settlers had quadrupled. Sea trade and fishing

Sunset on Key West's Mallory Square attracts a full spectrum of Keys residents and visitors

had become the businesses of the Keys and Key West was the place to live. On the fringes were a few farmers, raising crops of pineapple, coconuts and limes. Access changes everything, and for the Keys it came in the form of the railroad. Henry Flagler built his railroad for tourism, and that has been the focus of the Keys since the inaugural train trip arrived in Key West on January 22, 1912.

Today about 80,000 people live in the Florida Keys, nearly one third of them in Key West. The year 2000 census showed a mix of about 77% Caucasian, 16% Hispanic, 5% Black or African-American and 2% other races. Those who are not retired mostly work in the diving/fishing/tourism market, entertaining about four million visitors per year.

LANGUAGE

English is the principal language in the Florida Keys. Many shops also have staff who speak Spanish. Other languages may be available as well, but calling a shop's toll-free number or an internet search are probably the best ways to find out in advance.

Charter boats wait in the Florida sun for the day's visiting fishermen

Diver and fish meet at a coral and sponge-covered ridge off Key Largo

Clear blue water and abundant shallow coral make diving and snorkeling a pleasure in the Keys

Diving in the Keys

Deep water sea fans and elephant ear sponges decorate an arch on the reef

The Florida Keys encompass 100 miles of coral reef stretched out in a long arc along the Atlantic. Throw in the reefs off Biscayne Bay to the north and down to the Dry Tortugas in the south and you've got 200 miles of diving. Most of it is in the 20ft to 50ft (6m to 15m) range, and a lot is between the surface and 20ft (6m). There are some very nice sections of the reef in the 50ft to 80ft (15m to 24m) range, and quite a few of the wrecks occupy a profile from 50ft to 130ft (15m to 40m). If you're a member of the technical diving community, you can even find some great dives well below the sport diving limit, although those are not covered in this book. The point of this description is that the Keys have something for every diver, from novice to expert.

Since the reefs are located anywhere from two to six nautical miles off shore, all diving is by boat. The ride out to the reefs can take 20 to 45 minutes, depending on the type of boat and the distance to the dive site. Nearly all shops offer four dives each day: two in the morning and two in the afternoon. A night dive is usually offered once a week, sometimes twice.

The conditions that affect diving in the Keys are somewhat different than other parts of the world. The Gulf Stream, for instance, plays a major role in visibility. If the stream is close to the reefs, divers enjoy sparkling blue water, regardless of wind or tide. Visibility is normally in the 40ft to 70ft range (12m to 21m) on the outer reefs, but can be higher or lower from location to location. In general, the outer reefs offer better visibility than the inner reefs. In the lower Keys, where numerous cuts allow free flow of water from bayside to oceanside, the visibility tends to fluctuate daily with the tide. In the upper Keys, where longer island masses tend to limit water flow from bay to ocean, the visibility tends to fluctuate on longer cycles with the position of the Gulf Stream.

With no landmass to shelter the reefs, high winds can make things uncomfortable on the surface in some locations. Any day can be flat and calm, but the trade winds are more likely to be blowing in winter than in the summer. In general, low wind conditions are common from May to October, with a higher chance of wind from November to April.

Of course, the presence of a tropical storm can change everything. The hurricane season runs from the start of June to the end of November, with most storms occurring in late August, September and the first half of October. One of the ironies of diving in south Florida is that some of the best diving is during the hurricane season, provided there is not actually a storm about to hit.

Generally dives are not guided in the Florida Keys. A briefing is conducted at each site and dive pairs are free to explore at their own pace. Guided dives are usually available if desired, but ex-pect to make arrangements in advance and pay an additional fee. Captains normally choose the site based on a consensus from the boat, coupled with their own experience about where the best conditions can be found. Deeper dives, especially wrecks, are made first. Some boats limit bottom time on the shallower second dive to 45 minutes or an hour, as a courtesy to others and to keep on schedule.

Diving in the Florida Keys is like diving in a big aquarium packed with fish. Nearly half a century of protective management has helped keep an abundant fish population in place, even though the live coral cover has declined somewhat. The signature image of a dive in the Keys is probably a school of grunts, hanging shoulder to shoulder in the water and eyeing the camera from only a few feet away. The magic of diving here is seeing all those and more – snapper, jacks, damselfish, angelfish, surgeonfish, trumpetfish, butterflyfish…

Upper Keys' dive boat on mooring

Best Reef

The list of contenders for this honor includes such long-time favorites as **Molasses,** the **Elbow** and **Looe Key,** but the title goes to **Western Sambo** for its ancient and still-healthy star coral colonies. A decade of additional protection as a Sanctuary Ecological Reserve has boosted the fish population, restoring this extensive reef system and its multiple dive sites to underwater glory.

Massive star coral colonies are found at Western Sambo

Best Drift

The deep section of **Molasses Reef** seems custom-made for drift diving. The 45ft to 75ft (14m to 23m) depth profile allows good bottom time and the sharp slope makes for interesting terrain. A good current is nearly always present, although you may be drifting south one day and north the next.

Best Night

Just about any shallow reef in the Keys will provide an enjoyable night dive, and there are dozens of them up and down the chain. The *Benwood* wreck is a consistent night dive favorite – it's shallow, fishy and critter-filled, plus it's easier than most reefs to navigate at night. The site is not terribly large and there are plenty of easy-to-remember landmarks to guide you back to the boat.

Best Wreck

The reefs of the Florida Keys have brought thousands of ships to grief over the centuries, so it's fitting that there should be so many great wrecks to dive today. The *Duane,* the *Thunderbolt,* the *Eagle* and the *Busch* are all wonderful dives, but the king daddy of them all has got to be the massive *Spiegel Grove.* Spectacular from the outside, the ship is well-perforated for diver penetrations. Just be sure you don't get in further than you can safely handle with your level of training and experience.

Best Critter

Slow your pace to a standstill and you'll find yourself in critter heaven nearly anyplace you dive in the Keys. The shallow wrecks are always good bets when it comes to marine invertebrates, and one of the best is **Flagler's Barge**. The combination of wreck structure and sand provides plenty of protected habitat and food, so this entire area is filled with critters. Bring your macro lens and waterproof guide, then settle in for an hour of non-stop discovery.

Tiny Christmas tree worms

WHAT TO BRING

Diving is year round in the Keys, with water temperatures varying from about 85°F (29°C) in the summer to about 73°F (23°C) in the winter. Visitors usually rent 3mm full suits in the winter and 3mm shorties in the spring, summer and fall. Diving with only a bathing suit or a bathing suit and a T-shirt is popular in the summer. Local divers tend to wear 5mm full wet suits in the winter and something very light, such as Lycra or a 1mm suit, in the summer.

K-valves and yoke-style regulators are the standard in the Keys. Some shops have a few DIN adaptors on hand, but don't count on it. If you have a DIN first stage and want to use your own regulator, bring your own adaptors. Nearly all dive operators provide tanks and weights as part of the package. Aluminum 80 cubic ft tanks pumped to 3000psi (plus or minus a bit) are most common and weights are generally

Divers can expect excellent conditions year-round in the Keys

Ocean Divers' 46ft Newton dive boat, a typical large Keys dive boat with amenities like open transom, double ladders, showers, marine toilet and abundant seating

Rating System for Dives & Divers

Glass-bottom boats let non-divers enjoy the reefs too

The dive sites in this book are rated according to the following system. These are not absolute ratings but apply to divers at a particular time, diving at a particular place. For instance, someone unfamiliar with prevailing conditions might be considered a novice diver at one dive area, and an intermediate diver at another, more familiar location.

Novice*
A novice diver generally fits the following profile:
- basic scuba certification from an internationally recognized certifying agency
- dives infrequently (less than one trip a year)
- logged fewer than 25 total dives
- little or no experience diving in similar waters and conditions
- dives no deeper than 60ft (18m)

*an instructor or divemaster should accompany a novice diver on all dives.

Intermediate
An intermediate diver generally fits the following profile:
- may have participated in some form of continuing diver education
- logged between 25 and 100 dives
- no deeper than 130ft (40m)
- has been diving in similar waters and conditions within the last six months

Advanced
An advanced diver generally fits the following profile:
- advanced certification
- has been diving for more than two years; logged over 100 dives
- has been diving in similar waters and conditions within the last six months

Pre-Dive Safety Guidelines
Regardless of skill level, you should be in good physical condition and know your limitations. If uncertain as to which category you fit, ask the advice of a local dive instructor. He or she is best qualified to assess your abilities based on the prevailing dive conditions at any given site. Ultimately you must decide if you are capable of making a particular dive, taking into acount your level of training, recent experience, and physical condition, as well as water conditions at the site.

Remember that water conditions can change at any time, even during a dive.

solid lead in 2lb, 3lb or 4lb sizes. Some shops have smaller tanks and lead shot weights available, but call ahead if you have to have it.

Nitrox is widely available, usually in 32%, for an extra fee. Bring your nitrox certification card. Some shops are equipped to service rebreathers as well.

Spare yourself the trouble of bringing spare gear in case yours breaks. You could show up with only a certification card and be totally outfitted with first-rate rental gear within minutes. The Keys have lots of repair, rental and retail outlets, so you can rent or replace almost any of your own dive gear. One possible exception is prescription

Green sea turtles are often encountered by divers and snorkelers in the Keys

masks. Traveling with a back-up is a good idea, although some shops have generic prescription masks in a variety of increments.

Remember to pack your certification card, because every shop will ask to see it. Verification can usually be obtained by fax from your certifying agency if you can't produce your card, but you're likely to miss a day or two of diving. Bring your logbook if you want to make any advanced dives, such as on the deep wrecks.

Casual is the dress code in the Florida Keys, although you may find couples in souvenir T-shirts dining next to people in expensive resort wear in fine restaurants. Day-to-day, most visitors are decked out in the three S's: shorts, shirts and sandals (or sneakers). A jacket or sweatshirt can be essential on a winter evening or when coming back from diving. A light rain jacket or portable umbrella can also come in handy.

Drug stores with well-supplied pharmacies are located throughout the Keys, but bringing a sufficient supply of your own prescription medicines is probably the best plan. Over-the-counter medicines for headaches, colds, congestion or other minor maladies are readily available.

Friendly fish are the Keys' finest resource

Step right in – the water's great!

DIVE TRAINING & CERTIFICATION

All of the major dive certification agencies, including PADI, NAUI, SSI, YMCA, BSAC, CMAS, IDEA, HSAI, ACUC and PDIC, are recognized in the Keys. For nitrox and other technical diving applications, IANTD, ANDI and TDI are also recognized. The Florida Keys are an excellent location to receive dive training, with instructor training centers located in the upper, middle and lower Keys. Year-round diving and on-site testing offer efficiencies that cannot be matched elsewhere.

DIVE OPERATORS

A peek at the listing section of this guide will show you that there are plenty of choices when it comes to diving in the Florida Keys. With very few exceptions, the quality of service is extremely high. People who visit the Keys frequently have their favorites, and most preferences revolve around style and size. Dive operators vary from small businesses whose sole asset is a six-passenger dive boat and tanks, to full-service businesses with several boats, a retail shop and a large staff. The style in general is pretty laid back – they'll take you out, brief you and let you do your own thing – but some are more personable than others.

If you want to check up on a dive operator before you arrive, check to see if they belong to either the Florida Keys Chambers of Commerce or the Florida Keys Association of Dive Operators (KADO). Both organizations insist on certain standards and can give you more information about any operator you may be considering. The Chambers of Commerce website can be found at www.florida-keys.fl.us/chamber.htm. The KADO website can be found at www.divekeys.com.

LIVE ABOARDS

Sea-Clusive Charters operates a three to four day trip to the Dry Tortugas out of Key West. Sea-Clusive's vessel is 60ft long and carries a maximum of 11 passengers in four air-conditioned staterooms. For more information call ☎ 305-744-9928 or check the website at www.seaclusive.com.

SNORKELING

Snorkeling is one of the Keys' most popular activities and there are many shallow reefs to enjoy with only mask, fins and snorkel. Even complete novices usually find themselves floating comfortably over the reef, fascinated by the incredible sea life after just a bit of instruction and help.

If you are only snorkeling, not diving, check first to be sure that your boat is going to sites that are suitable for snorkeling. Many reefs in the Keys are good for both diving and snorkeling, but not all of them. If you're on one of the boats that carry only snorkelers, of course this won't be a problem.

Snorkeling is most fun when the water is calm. If the wind is blowing, your captain can often find a spot that is well protected from the weather, but expect lower visibility. If it's really blowing hard, it might be a good day for land activities.

UNDERWATER PHOTOGRAPHY

Whether you're shooting digital stills, film or video, the Keys are an excellent location for underwater photography, with clear water and easily approachable marine life. Photo supplies, rental equipment and instruction are available at many dive shops. In the upper Keys, photographers are fortunate to have the services of world famous Stephen Frink Photographic to assist with their photo needs. The shop is located at MM 102.5 (bayside), Key Largo, FL 33037. Toll-free calling is available at ☎ 800-451-3737, or ☎ 305-451-3737. On the web, look for www.stephenfrink.com or email info@stephenfrink.com.

Novice or expert, underwater photographers love the Florida Keys

Parrotfish are among the hundreds of species you can see in the Keys

A massive globe of smooth brain coral greets divers descending toward the reef

Conservation

A series of ships sunk as artificial reefs provide habitat for sea creatures as well as fun for divers

Fort Jefferson National Monument was the first park in the Florida Keys, securing protection for the historic fort and surrounding waters in 1935. The park was renamed Dry Tortugas National Park in 1992. The next part of the coral reef ecosystem to be protected was the Everglades, which provides nursery grounds for many species and is an important source of fresh water. Everglades National Park was designated in 1947.

The reefs themselves though were pillaged for shells, tropical fish and coral in the 1950s, prompting creation of the John Pennekamp Coral Reef State Park in 1960, and for many divers the name Pennekamp is synonymous with marine conservation in the Florida Keys. John Pennekamp, former editor of *The Miami Herald,* and many others were instrumental in establishing a true marine park and raising awareness of the need for conservation. The original park was about 20 miles (32km) long and stretched from the shoreline out to a depth of 60ft (18m), approximately 5 miles (8km) offshore. A US Supreme Court ruling on another matter later reduced the state of Florida's jurisdiction to 3 miles (4.8km) offshore, leaving most of the reefs unprotected. The Key Largo National Marine Sanctuary was quickly designated to correct the problem, and coral reef protection off Key Largo extended seamlessly from the shore to a depth of 300ft (91m). Looe Key National Marine Sanctuary was set aside in 1981, bringing coral reef management to the Middle Keys.

In 1989 a series of ship groundings destroyed acres of coral, and officials realized the need for a more comprehensive marine park. Congress created the Florida Keys National Marine Sanctuary (FKNMS) the following year and gave the task of managing the sanctuary to the National Oceanic and Atmospheric Administration (NOAA). The FKNMS sanctuary plan was approved five years later, significantly spreading the umbrella of protection. A key feature of the plan was the zoning scheme, which created 18 sanctuary preservation areas (SPAs) to protect the most popular diving reefs, creating 'no-harvest' (including fishing) and 'no-disturbance' zones. The zoning also provides additional protection for 15 existing management areas under the Florida Department of Environmental Protection, four US Fish and Wildlife Service refuges and an ecological reserve devoted to marine life replenishment.

The whole system was put together by different people in different agencies at different times, but it's actually a cohesive conservation plan that provides both protection and access. Think of it this way: all of the Florida Keys are protected at the most basic level. No polluting, no dumping, no drilling, no damaging or removing coral. In selected areas, including many of the major reefs, that basic protection is expanded to include no fishing, no lobstering and no anchoring. A handful of additional areas are set aside for research or environmental recovery. In these few areas, access is limited or prohibited. The net result for divers and snorkelers is healthier reefs, more fish, and less conflict with fishermen and non-diving boaters. With so many agencies with separate and overlapping jurisdictions you may see officers and volunteers from the FKNMS, John Pennekamp Coral Reef State Park, the Florida Marine Patrol or the US Coast Guard. They're out there for you, so wave and say hello.

MARINE CONSERVATION ORGANIZATIONS

All of the Florida Keys, from Key Largo to the Dry Tortugas, are included in the FKNMS. Part of the US National Marine Sanctuary Program, this is a multiple use protected area with an overall goal of long-term conservation. For more information, contact the FKNMS by email at floridakeys@noaa.gov or visit the website at www.floridakeys.noaa.gov.

Several other important federal and state protected areas exist within, or adjacent to, the FKNMS. The best known by divers is John Pennekamp Coral Reef State Park, but the Florida Park Service also maintains Long Key State Park, Bahia Honda State Park, Windley Key Fossil Reef Geological State Park, Lignumvitae Key Botanical State Park,

Shell & Coral Products

Shallow growing elkhorn and antler corals are easily broken by careless snorkelers, divers or boaters

Removing shells or coral from the waters of the Florida Keys National Marine Sanctuary is not allowed, regardless of whether they are living or dead. If you must have a shell or coral souvenir, the Overseas Hwy (US1) has a number of shops like Shell World that offer such things. The store-bought items are legal because they come from overseas locations such as the Philippines, but doesn't stripping someplace else while preserving the Keys seem a bit hypocritical?

What not to do in the Keys – no standing on the coral please!

Dagny Johnson Key Largo Hammock Botanical State Park, Fort Zachary Taylor Historic State Park and the Indian Key Historic State Park. For more information, visit the Florida Park Service website at www.dep.state.fl.us/parks.

Two major parks in the National Park Service system, Everglades and Biscayne Bay, provide essential protection to large areas surrounding the FKNMS. More information on Everglades National Park and Biscayne National Park can be found at www.nps.gov/ever and www.nps.gov/bisc respectively.

The US Fish and Wildlife Service maintains three vital wildlife refuges within the FKNMS, including Crocodile Lake National Wildlife Refuge, the Key West National Wildlife Refuge and the Great White Heron National Wildlife Refuge. For more information, see the USFWS website at www.fws.gov/refuges.

Reef Relief is a non-profit volunteer organization dedicated to the preservation of the Florida Keys and other coral reef ecosystems. More information on Reef Relief can be obtained at their website, www.reefrelief.org.

Reef Environmental Education Foundation (REEF) is another non-profit volunteer organization, devoted to preserving the marine environment primarily through conducting underwater surveys of fish and invertebrates. View their website at www.reef.org.

RESPONSIBLE DIVING

The most important rules for responsible diving are basically common sense:
- do not touch, stand on, kick, break or remove coral
- do not remove, damage or disturb scientific equipment or historical artifacts
- do not run aground on the reefs or injure seagrass with your boat
- do not anchor in coral or allow your anchor chain or line to contact coral.
- display a dive flag when diving or snorkeling
- operate at idle speed within 100 yards (91m) of dive flags.

For a complete listing of sanctuary regulations, check with the FKNMS at www.floridakeys.noaa.gov.

Encrusting sponges and corals light up the
Florida Keys reefs with dramatic colors

Health & Safety

The Florida Keys present little health risk; in fact the main danger is from the sun. Proper hydration, the liberal use of a SPF15 or higher sunscreen and a broad-brimmed hat should suffice to prevent problems in this regard. Although mosquito-born diseases are not prevalent, mosquitoes and small gnats (called no-see-ums) can be annoying, especially during calm summer evenings. Insect repellent is available throughout the Keys if needed.

Crime is not a big problem in the Keys, but common sense precautions are a good idea. Lock unattended automobiles and do not leave dive gear or cameras in plain sight.

The Overseas Highway is a lovely scenic road, but it can be frustratingly slow at times. If you experience a back-up, relax and go with the flow (or lack of it) rather than losing patience.

PRE-DEPARTURE PLANNING

A surprisingly large proportion of the divers visiting the Keys have not been in the water in a number of years, sometimes many years. If you haven't dived in a while, it might be a good idea to have your gear serviced before you go. Short one-on-one refresher courses are available nearly everywhere in the Keys to knock the rust off your diving skills before you head for the reefs.

Crime is not prevalent in the Keys, but common-sense says keep your eye on your belongings

If you're going to rent a boat, make sure your navigational skills are up to par

Some reefs, like this one in the Dry Tortugas, are far from shore, so carrying a signaling device is prudent

A diver can be extremely difficult to locate in the water, so always dive with a signaling device of some sort, preferably more than one.

One of the best signaling devices and the easiest to carry is a whistle. Use a zip tie to attach one permanently to your BC. Even better, though more expensive, is a loud air horn that connects to the inflator hose. You simply push a button to let out a blast. It does require air from your tank to function, though.

A great visual device to carry with you is a marker tube, also known as a safety sausage. The best ones are brightly colored and about 10ft (3m) high. These roll up and easily fit into a BC pocket or clip onto a D-ring. They're inflated orally or with a regulator. Some will allow you to insert a dive light into the tube – a useful feature when it's dark.

Consider carrying at least a small light with you at all times – not just night diving. It can be unexpectedly useful during the day for looking into rocky crevices and will come in handy as a signaling device as daylight fades. Some lights feature a strobe option for signaling.

Watch your depth and bottom time, especially on the deep wrecks where it can be easy to get distracted

MEDICAL & RECOMPRESSION FACILITIES

Health-care in the Florida Keys has improved significantly over the past decade. Residents and visitors now enjoy high-quality care at new or recently updated facilities in Tavernier, Marathon and Key West. Extensive health-care facilities are also available in Miami.

DAN

Divers Alert Network (DAN) is an international membership association of individuals and organizations sharing a common interest in scuba diving and safety. DAN operates a 24-hour diving emergency hotline, for members and non-members. Although DAN does not directly provide medical care, it does give advice on early treatment, evacuation, and hyperbaric treatment of diving-related injuries.

Reef fish will let you get very close in the Florida Keys

DAN often receives requests for information and contact numbers for recompression chambers by divers who think it may be in their best interest to know the number and location of the nearest recompression chamber. Although this information may be helpful, it often compromises dive safety by creating the impression that rushing an injured diver to the nearest chamber is the most important consideration in an emergency. This is not often the case and may even be dangerous. The nearest hyperbaric chamber may not always be the best suited to treat a particular diving emergency. Also, many hyperbaric chambers are not set up to provide a 24-hour service and it may take some time in getting together a hyperbaric team ready to treat an injured diver. It has happened more than once that an injured diver has been rushed to a recompression chamber only to find the facility closed or even out of service. Several facilities only have access to a

Diving & Flying

Many divers in the Florida Keys arrive by plane. While it's fine to dive soon after flying, it's important to remember that your last dive should be completed at least 24 hours before your flight to minimize the risk of decompression sickness, caused by residual nitrogen in the blood.

single doctor trained in treating recompression illness. When this person is absent, there may be no-one able to handle the casualty.

In addition, divers with serious symptoms may not necessarily have decompression illness. They may be suffering from a heart attack, stroke or some other medical disorder. Therefore, rather than blindly rushing a diver in distress to a hyperbaric center, it may be more appropriate to take them to the nearest 24-hour emergency room first. The ER staff can obtain a more detailed assessment of the problem, establish a diagnosis and provide adequate stabilization.

DAN therefore does not provide information on recompression chambers to divers on request and encourages injured divers to be given immediate emergency first aid and 100% oxygen, and be taken to the nearest 24-hour emergency room as quickly as possible.

For a diving emergency in the Florida Keys, call local EMS first, then call DAN EMERGENCY HOTLINE AT ☎ 1-919-684-8111. Medically trained DAN personnel will help assess the situation and make the additional transport arrangements if needed, by providing evacuation or referral information to a local diving physician. The caller will be required to provide contact telephone number and names, details of the location and information pertaining to the emergency. You can also contact DAN by calling collect at ☎ 1-919-684-4(DAN).

DAN strongly suggests any diver facing a medical emergency follow these steps:

1 Address any life-threatening situations first. Keep the injured diver in a horizontal position and carry out Cardio Pulmonary Resuscitation (CPR) if necessary.
2 Administer 100% Oxygen for as long as possible, ensuring that the injured diver is breathing adequately. If not, provide mouth-to-mouth or equipment-assisted ventilation.
3 Provide oral fluids only if the injured diver is fully conscious and able to drink unaided.
4 Call the DAN EMERGENCY HOTLINE at ☎ 1-919-684-8111 for advice, assistance and evacuation as needed. DAN will make the necessary arrangements and liaise with health-care professionals managing the diving emergency to facilitate appropriate treatment of the injured diver.

5 If possible, transport the injured diver to the nearest 24-hour casualty center.
6 Take the DAN Oxygen Provider Course to understand and be confident in the administration of emergency oxygen first aid. Contact DAN toll-free at ☎ 1-800-446-2671 for more information.

Membership is reasonably priced and includes DAN TravelAssist, which covers medical air evacuation from anywhere in the world for illness or injury. Lack of this, or similar, coverage can slow rescue operations while payment is sorted out. Please note: To access the TravelAssist benefits, DAN must be contacted in the event of medical emergency requiring evacuation.

For a small additional fee, divers can get secondary insurance coverage for scuba diving injuries. For membership questions, contact DAN toll-free at ☎ 1-800-446-2671 in the USA, and ☎ 1-919-684-2948 elsewhere. More information is also available on the internet at www.diversalertnetwork.org.

Medical Contacts

Mariners Hospital
(MM 91.5, Tavernier; ☎ 304-852-4418)
On-site recompression chamber.
Fishermen's Hospital
(3301 Overseas Hwy, Marathon;
☎ 305-743-5533) No chamber.
Lower Keys Medical Center
(5900 College Rd, Stock Island;
☎ 305-294-5531)
ER physicians may refer emergency decompression sickness cases to Key West military recompression chamber.
Mercy Hospital
(3663 South Miami Ave, Miami, FL 33133; ☎ 305-854-4400)
Two recompression chambers.
For 24 hour recompression questions call ☎ 800-NO-BENDS (800-662-3637)

Slow ascents help keep decompression problems away

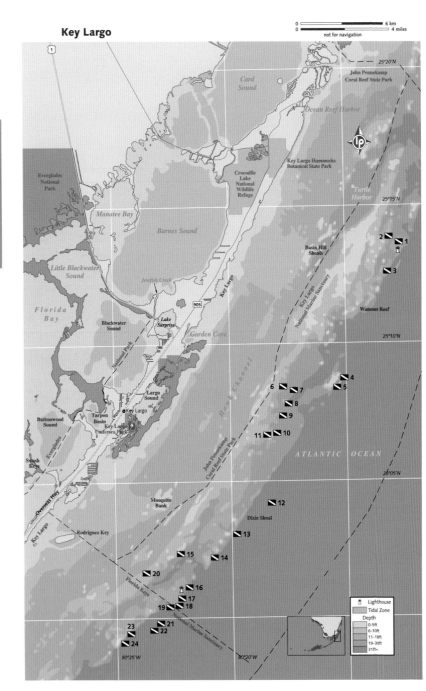

Key Largo

0 ————— 6 km
0 ————— 4 miles
not for navigation

Key Largo & the Upper Keys

Carysfort Light has been guarding this reef since 1852

magnificent open-framework structure literally screwed to the top of the reef, was constructed. The tower stands 112ft high, with quarters for the lighthouse keeper and assistant. It was manned until 1960, and remains an active automated navigational marker today.

Blue water is the exception rather than the rule at Carysfort, but the green tint does little to detract from the quality of the diving. The big star and brain coral heads attract scores of reef fish. Larger animals, including turtles, rays and sharks, are frequently encountered by divers here in the shadow of the old reef light.

1 CARYSFORT REEF (FORE)

Location: *6 nautical miles (11km) southeast of Ocean Reef Harbor*
Depth Range: *Surface-60ft (18m)*
Access: *Boat*
Expertise Rating: *Intermediate*

Historically, Carysfort may be the most significant reef in the upper Keys. It's been the site of countless groundings over the years, including HMS *Carysford,* which ran aground here on October 23, 1770. Somewhere along the way Carysford was changed to Carysfort, a small detail that was probably not important to other ships that came to grief on the reef. The number of disasters grew so large that a lightship was eventually stationed off the reef in 1825 to warn mariners. In 1852 the present lighthouse, a

Key Largo & the Upper Keys	GOOD SNORKELING	NOVICE	INTERMEDIATE	ADVANCED
1 CARYSFORT REEF (FORE)	•		•	
2 CARYSFORT REEF (BACK)	•	•		
3 SOUTH CARYSFORT REEF	•		•	
4 CITY OF WASHINGTON	•	•		
5 ELBOW REEF	•		•	
6 HORSESHOE REEF	•	•		
7 NORTH NORTH DRY ROCKS	•	•		
8 NORTH DRY ROCKS	•	•		
9 KEY LARGO DRY ROCKS	•	•		
10 GRECIAN ROCKS (FORE REEF)	•	•		
11 GRECIAN ROCKS (BACK REEF)	•	•		
12 SPIEGEL GROVE				•
13 BENWOOD		•		
14 FRENCH REEF	•		•	
15 WHITE BANK	•	•		
16 SAND ISLAND	•		•	
17 MOLASSES REEF (NORTH)	•		•	
18 MOLASSES REEF (DEEP)				•
19 MOLASSES REEF (SOUTH)	•		•	
20 THREE SISTERS	•	•		
21 BIBB				•
22 DUANE				•
23 PILLAR CORAL PATCH	•		•	
24 PICKLES	•		•	

One unusual feature of Carysfort Reef is the fossil reef formation at 55ft. A second spur-and-groove formation lies at this depth, the site of an ancient reef that was 'drowned' as water levels rose thousands of years ago. It's less well-defined than the shallower living reef, but it's still easy to spot. This deeper part of the reef features a greater concentration of sponge life than the shallower sections, as well as many soft corals and low profile hard corals.

2 CARYSFORT REEF (BACK)

Location: *6 nautical miles (11km) southeast of Ocean Reef Harbor*
Depth Range: *Surface-10ft (3m)*
Access: *Boat*
Expertise Rating: *Novice*

The extensive elkhorn and antler corals that once dominated the shallow top of Carysfort reef have declined over the years, but this is still an excellent snorkel area. Most of the time it's protected from the wind by the shallow bulk of the reef, providing flat water even during a pretty good blow. Both the living and the fossilized portions of the reef top continue to attract lots of fish, which find food and shelter among its many crevices. With reasonably deep water behind the reef, snorkelers can swim right beside the shallow edge of the coral and enjoy a close-up view of its inhabitants.

Surgeonfish, damselfish and parrotfish are the main families of reef fish you'll find here. The reason for that is simple: abundant food. All of these species graze either directly on the coral or on algae growing on the coral. In fact, some damselfish even tend their own little gardens of algae on the coral, particularly on blades of fossilized elkhorn. Linger too long near one of these algae

farms and the tiny damselfish won't hesitate to come right out and shoo you away.

If you're visiting the reef on a calm day, stop and listen for a minute. One of the things you'll discover is that the so-called 'silent world' is anything but silent. Listen closely and you may actually hear the scraping noise of parrotfish munching on the coral. With beak-like jaws they tear into the coral like a hungry cowboy ripping into a steak at a BBQ. After they've digested the coral polyps and algae, only the calcium carbonate skeleton of the coral remains – basically sand. This they excrete, adding a significant amount of sand to the bottom each year.

Use caution swimming over the top of the reef at this site as it is quite shallow, meaning you could get caught far from your boat as the tide changes and be faced with a long swim around the reef.

3 SOUTH CARYSFORT REEF

Location: *6.5 nautical miles (12km) southeast of Ocean Reef Harbor*
Depth Range: *Surface-80ft (24m)*
Access: *Boat*
Expertise Rating: *Intermediate*

Only a few decades ago the shallows of South Carysfort Reef were filled with exquisite live antler and elkhorn colonies. Storms and perhaps human activity have taken a toll, but all is not lost. Pockets of the original colonies remain intact and new colonies have already taken root.

Fortunately, these two species of branching coral are among the fastest growing in the world. Under the right conditions, elkhorn can grow 4in to 6in per year, a rate that allows it to recover rather quickly as far as corals go. That's

Elkhorn coral, a delicate branching coral that grows well in shallow water

Wreck of the City of Washington, Elbow Reef

a good thing, because it likes to grow in the 'danger zone,' where there is a lot of wave action and high surge.

Mooring buoys line both sides of the reef. The back reef buoys are convenient for snorkeling and are more protected when the wind is strong out of the northeast or east. The front reef buoys are good for snorkeling too, but they'll also put you in a good position for scuba diving. The depth near the front buoys is around 30ft, and you can head seaward, working your way down a gradual slope to 50ft or 60ft, or head landward toward the reef crest.

Divers generally start toward the deeper water, where the large star and giant star coral formations between the buoys and the reef crest form several arches and swim-throughs. Rather than hang on a line twiddling your thumbs while you do a five minute safety stop,

you can continue exploring the coral up toward the reef crest at the end of your dive.

4	CITY OF WASHINGTON

Location: *6 nautical miles (11km) east southeast of Garden Cove*
Depth Range: *15-25ft (5-8m)*
Access: *Boat*
Expertise Rating: *Novice*

The *City of Washington's* career was one of unexciting service carrying passengers and cargo between New York and Cuba, at least until the night of February 15, 1898. That night she happened to be anchored next to the battleship USS *Maine* when the ship exploded in

Black grouper on the City of Washington

Havana harbor. The *City of Washington's* crew rescued 90 sailors from the tragedy. Although the cause of the explosion is still debated, it marked the start of the Spanish-American War, a conflict in which the *City of Washington* served as a troop ship.

She was built by the shipyard of John Roach and Sons in Pennsylvania in 1877 as a two-masted sailing vessel, 320ft long with a 38ft beam. Two years later she was taken back to the yard and fitted with a 2750hp steam engine. In 1908 her engine was removed, and the ship was converted to a coal barge. While under tow by the tugboat *Edgar F. Luckenbach,* the *City of Washington* struck the reef and sank. The wreckage was later considered a hazard to navigation and was dynamited. The basic hull form, consisting of the lower bilge section, is still intact, but the other parts of the ship have been reduced to large pieces of metal plate. The maximum depth on the wreck is 25ft.

Great barracuda and green moray eels have been hand fed at this site for many years, acclimating them to contact with divers. Don't be alarmed if you suddenly find one about 4in from your mask, expectantly looking you in the eye. Curl your fingers up so they won't be mistaken for small baitfish, and keep your hands by your sides.

The wreck of the *City of Washington* is a superb night dive. Its shallow depth makes it perfect for the last dive of the day, and navigation is easy because you can just stay on or near the wreck. Try diving the wreck during the day and then again at night. The difference is quite literally night and day, with new colors, new fish life and a completely different experience.

5   ELBOW REEF

Location: *6 nautical miles (11km) east southeast of Garden Cove*
Depth Range: *15-85ft (5-26m)*
Access: *Boat*
Expertise Rating: *Intermediate*

If you fly over the Florida Keys and look straight down, you'll see that the Elbow Reef is not exactly in line with the other reefs. It sticks out to seaward a bit, like an elbow, of course. Sticking out like that means the Elbow Reef is first to benefit when the clear, blue waters of the Gulf Stream shift closer to Florida than to the Bahamas. As a result the Elbow nearly always has good visibility.

One of the disadvantages of poking out further than the other reefs is that the Elbow was hit by ships fairly frequently. The remains of several wrecks litter the reef, including the *City of Washington,* the Civil War Wreck and the *Tonawanda,* a steamer that sank here in 1866. Mike's Wreck, a steel vessel of unknown origin, can also be seen here, with several large sections of the hull in about 25ft.

The depth is about 15ft over the shallowest coral ridges at the Elbow, which slope in a fairly even gradient toward deep water. The prominent ridges end in 30ft to 35ft of water, and the bottom is more uniformly flat, although as you move into deeper water, you'll pick up vestiges of the coral ridges and sand channels. For some reason turtle encounters, mostly with hawksbills and loggerheads, are frequent on the Elbow, particularly below 30ft.

One deeper mooring buoy sits atop the southern reef section. The depth is just below 50ft at the buoy, and the bottom slopes very gradually toward a lip at 55ft called 'Nelson's Ledge.' The terrain slopes more steeply from this point, ending with scattered corals on a sand bottom in 85ft.

This area is characterized by prolific soft corals, lower-profile star and brain corals, many tube and finger sponges and large numbers of giant barrel sponges. These sponges, along with other species such as brown tube sponges and orange elephant ear sponges, attract large numbers of angelfish, which feed primarily on sponges. Queen, French and gray angelfish are particularly abundant.

Fish Feeding

While not technically banned, fish feeding is 'officially discouraged' within the boundaries of the Florida Keys National Marine Sanctuary. Fortunately, most visitors abide by the no feeding guidance, resulting in the large schools of snapper, grunts, jacks and goatfish that behave naturally and make diving in the Keys so enjoyable.

If you'd like to see fish being fed by humans, try one of Captain Slate's 'critter dives' at **Elbow Reef**. Continuing an historic tradition begun half a century ago by Keys diving pioneer Steve Klem, Captain Slate feeds nurse sharks and green moray eels by hand, then caps off the show by letting a barracuda streak in to snatch a ballyhoo held between his teeth. It will be an up-close-and-personal experience with these animals that you wouldn't get otherwise.

Reefs where large numbers of snorkelers gather – such as **Key Largo Dry Rocks** off Key Largo, or **Sand Key** off Key West – tend to have frenzied mobs of Bermuda chub and sergeant majors that result from feeding, since there are always a few who can't resist. It's fun for the casual tourist, but anyone with a stronger interest in the reefs will probably prefer the more natural settings away from such crowds.

Lightning whelk

6 HORSESHOE REEF

Location: *4 nautical miles (7.6km) southeast of Garden Cove and North Sound Creek*
Depth Range: *6-22 ft (2-7m)*
Access: *Boat*
Expertise Rating: *Novice*

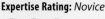

Horseshoe Reef is an excellent choice when there are both divers and snorkelers in the boat. This is one of the middle reefs, not quite shallow enough to be a true patch reef, but well back from the outer edge of the reef line where the deeper reefs are found. The horseshoe shape from which the reef takes its name can be found at the northern end of the reef, but the overall shape of the reef is a long, fairly straight line running north and south. To the east, or seaward, is a flat sandy plain with seagrass beds. The maximum depth is about 20ft in this area. The reef rises rather abruptly from the sand, made up principally of large star and brain coral colonies. The top of the reef is shallow, varying between about 5ft and 10ft

deep. Another sand and seagrass flat defines the western (landward) side of the reef, but the water is only 10ft to 12ft deep on this side.

A nice way to see this reef is by cruising along the seaward face in the deeper water, then returning to your boat along the top of the reef. There are lots of nooks and crannies to explore along the way in both directions, with abundant fish life. In the summer months, the overhangs may be packed with swirling silversides, which draw packs of marauding jacks to hunt the reef.

Don't ignore the seagrass beds adjacent to the reef just because they look uninteresting at first glance. During a brief excursion away from the reef face you may find lightning whelks, helmet conch, sand dollars, southern stingrays, spiny lobster and many other creatures.

Horseshoe Reef is a reasonable alternative if high winds are making the outer reefs uncomfortable, but expect lower visibility than usual as the sand around the reef gets stirred up. When the seas are flat and the blue water slides in close to shore, Horseshoe can be one of the loveliest shallow reefs in the Keys.

7 NORTH NORTH DRY ROCKS

Location: *4.5 nautical miles (8.6km)*
southeast of Garden Cove
Depth Range: *5-25 ft (2-8m)*
Access: *Boat*
Expertise Rating: *Novice*

North North Dry Rocks is a fish watcher's delight. It's a great location to see all five of the Keys' angelfish family, including the ubiquitous gray angelfish, the black and yellow French angelfish, the elegant blue angelfish and the brilliantly colored queen angelfish. The fifth member of the clan is the rock beauty, a smaller and sometimes shy angelfish that is easily recognized by its bright yellow head and black body.

Even though you see a lot of them here, angelfish make up only a small portion of the fish population of North North Dry Rocks. Any of the Florida Keys'

fish species could turn up, but some of the other common species here include the trumpetfish, surgeonfish, scrawled filefish, smooth trunkfish, yellow stingrays and spotted morays. Look under the ledges and you may also see small schools of copper sweepers circling in the shadows.

The shallow depths found here give divers plenty of bottom time, and even lets snorkelers view the reef and fish life while floating on the surface. In fact, use caution when entering the water, in case your boat happens to swing over one of the shallower sections of the reef. An enthusiastic giant stride could bring your heels close to the coral.

The reef consists of a series of coral fingers separated by sandy channels. During the last couple of thousand years, generations of coral polyps have built the fingers up to an impressive height, high enough that divers may prefer to go around the ends rather than cross over the top, in order to avoid a lot of up and down profiling.

Dive Boats

Dive boats in the Florida Keys are among the highest quality to be found anywhere in the world. There are several reasons why this is so, starting with stringent safety requirements of the US Coast Guard. Every dive boat is under the command of a Coast Guard certified captain, who stays on the boat to continually watch over its safe operation. In addition to the safety requirements, competition keeps the Florida Keys boats in top shape. The best looking and most comfortable boats get the best business, so visiting divers enjoy the finest boats available.

As all the boats are well-crewed and in excellent condition, the main criterion for choosing a boat is size, with the choices being small, large and in-between. The small boats are certified for six passengers maximum, and are commonly called 'six packs.' The obvious advantage of these smaller boats is that you're not diving with a crowd. The six pack boats can also be a bit more flexible than the larger boats on where they go. The downside is that few of the small boats have amenities like marine toilets and freshwater showers and when high winds stir up the waves, the ride can be rough.

The large boats ride better in most conditions and offer more seating choices, more elbow room and more amenities. The downside is that you may be out there with 30 or 40 other divers. That doesn't necessarily mean you'll be bumping into people underwater – if you relax and let the first rush hit the water, there's plenty of time to get in and see the reef quietly.

In-between small and large are boats that typically accommodate 10 to 20 divers.

Smooth trunkfish

8   NORTH DRY ROCKS

Location: *4.5 nautical miles (8.6km) southeast of Garden Cove*
Depth Range: *5-25ft (2-8m)*
Access: *Boat*
Expertise Rating: *Novice*

Also known as 'Minnow Cave' by some dive operators North Dry Rocks is another of the inner bank reefs that is well suited to both diving and snorkeling.

The tops of the coral ridges are barely 5ft below the surface, so snorkelers can float along without diving down and still enjoy the fish life.

For divers, North Dry Rocks is like an underwater maze. Even though it's a small reef, getting turned around is easy. At least the boat isn't far away when you get lost here.

Like **North North Dry Rocks**, the coral ridges here have a very high profile, effectively dividing one passage from another unless you swim over the top or around the end. Near the middle of the reef, a large archway is often filled to overflowing with silversides (also called glass minnows) during the summer months, giving the reef its second name of Minnow Cave. The seaward ends of the ridges are capped with a magnificent buttress of huge star coral formations.

Reefs like North Dry Rocks are good alternates when high winds increase the wave action, making the outer reefs uncomfortable. Expect lower visibility at such times, though, as the waves stir up the bottom. It's still a good dive, even if the visibility isn't sparkling.

Christ of the Deep, a 9ft tall bronze statue at Key Largo Dry Rocks

9 KEY LARGO DRY ROCKS

Location: *4.5 nautical miles (8.6km) southeast of Garden Cove*
Depth Range: *Surface-30ft (9m)*
Access: *Boat*
Expertise Rating: *Novice*

This popular reef is also called simply 'Dry Rocks,' an indication that portions of it are exposed at low tide. Located slightly back from the line of outer reefs, Key Largo Dry Rocks is termed an 'inner bank reef' and displays characteristics of both bank reefs and patch reefs. The reef is roughly oval in shape, with the seaward portion being made up of spurs of coral separated by grooves of sand. The deepest part of the reef, about 30ft, can be found in the sand seaward of these spurs. On the landward side of the reef the coral is densely packed, essentially eliminating the sandy grooves.

The 9ft tall, 4000lb statue of Christ is on the seaward side, near a floating spar buoy. The statue is one of at least three cast from a mold by Italian sculptor Guido Galletti. The first, called *Christ of the Abyss*, was placed in 50ft of water off Genoa. A second casting was made in 1961 and presented to the people of Grenada for their assistance in rescuing passengers from a fire aboard the Italian liner *Bianca C*. That statue is on display in St George's Harbour in Grenada.

This statue, the third casting, was originally made for Egidi Cressi, whose company manufactures dive equipment. Cressi eventually donated the statue to the Underwater Society of America, who in turn passed it to the Florida Board of Parks and Historic Memorials for display. In the spring of 1966 Ellison Hardee, the first superintendent of John Pennekamp Coral Reef State Park, organized the effort to install the statue on its massive concrete pedestal at Key Largo Dry Rocks. Several months later Hurricane Betsy roared across Key Largo, but the statue was not damaged and remains intact today. Until about 10 years ago, volunteers scrubbed the statue regularly, to prevent overgrowth by sponges, algae or coral. Current marine sanctuary policy is to let the statue be overgrown, so each year its features are less discernable.

10 GRECIAN ROCKS (FORE REEF)

Location: *5 nautical miles (9.5km) southeast of Garden Cove*
Depth Range: *Surface-30ft (9m)*
Access: *Boat*
Expertise Rating: *Novice*

The north end of Grecian Rocks is reported to be the location where the opening credits of the 60s television show *Flipper* were filmed. Featuring the exploits of Ranger Ricks, his two sons Sandy and Bud, and of course Flipper, the show did much to popularize diving in the Keys.

Grecian is known as an inner bank reef, and is about a mile in from the main reef line. The reef profile on the seaward side is an abbreviated version of the spur-and-groove formation found on the outer reefs. The fore reef is a moderately steep slope, starting near the surface and descending to about 25ft near the mooring buoys. The bottom levels out in flat sand at 28ft to 30ft, with scattered clumps of coral trailing away from the reef. Mostly fossilized branching corals in the shallows give way to mixed hard and soft corals in the midsection and larger hard corals near the bottom. Fossil coral ridges are exposed in many places, with only a light covering of live coral.

Grecian Rocks is a Sanctuary Preservation Area (SPA), which affords it

Exploring 510ft of 'super wreck' is going to take more than one dive

added protection against damage to corals and seagrass, as well as a prohibition against fishing. The populations of reef and predatory fish on Grecian have grown appreciably since the SPA was designated in July 1997. Expect to see almost any of the common Keys reef fish here.

The mooring buoys wrap around the south side of the reef, where a cut forms a deep pass through the corals. The reef south of the pass is sometimes called 'Banana Reef.' Although it is slightly shallower, Banana Reef is similar to Grecian Rocks.

11 GRECIAN ROCKS (BACK REEF)

Location: *5 nautical miles (9.5km) southeast of Garden Cove*
Depth Range: *Surface-6ft (2m)*
Access: *Boat*
Expertise Rating: *Novice*

On windy days the back reef at Grecian Rocks is the last refuge for divers and snorkelers, as the broad, shallow reef provides an excellent lee. On calm days

Boat Navigation

As visitors often discover, navigating is not easy in the Florida Keys. The water is shallow, the land is flat and navigation markers are difficult to see. Add the sun's glare on the water and the results can be disastrous. Here are some tips that might help:
- buy large-scale charts and study them carefully before you venture out
- ask locals about the best routes to and from sites you want to visit
- don't follow your GPS blindly – it could be leading you over a shallow reef
- learn 'eyeball navigation,' the art of reading the water to avoid shallow areas
- wear polarizing sunglasses to help you read the bottom as well as possible
- if in doubt, slow down or stop. Re-orient yourself, plan a new route, then proceed.

12   SPIEGEL GROVE

Location: *4 nautical miles (7.5km) east of Mosquito Bank light*
Depth Range: *50-130ft (15-39m)*
Access: *Boat*
Expertise Rating: *Advanced*

Few wrecks have come to rest in as many positions as the *Spiegel Grove*. On May 17, 2002, she was upside down. On June 10, 2002, she landed on her starboard side. On July 9, 2005, she decided to turn upright and that's the way she now sits. It's certainly been interesting, but nearly everyone agrees this last position is by far the best.

This is one enormous wreck, so don't expect to see it all on one dive – or even on 10 dives. Built in Pascagoula, Mississippi, in 1954, she is 510ft long and 84ft wide. A pair of steam turbines generating 23,000hp could drive the ship at 21 knots (39km/h). The *Spiegel Grove* could carry 21 landing craft and eight helicopters, as well as 300 combat troops.

The massive hull rises from around 130ft on the bottom to about 50ft, providing a towering vertical profile. The superstructure is as big as an office building, the cranes are enormous and all the dive boats in Key Largo could be docked in the well deck together.

The interior, at least above the main deck, has been well-prepped for diver penetrations, with exits cut into the

it can still draw a crowd, because it's such a perfect spot for anyone taking their first look through a dive mask. The maximum depth behind the reef is 6ft, but much of the site is 4ft or less. The bottom is mostly sand and beds of turtle grass. At the back edge of the reef is a narrow rubble zone beside the coral shelf that delineates the reef crest. Wave action and high visitor impact have reduced the live coral cover on the reef crest, but it's still an interesting area. This is the reef that was meant to be called Key Largo Dry Rocks, which would have been a more fitting name since parts of the reef may be more than a foot out of the water at low tide.

First-time snorkelers are usually captivated by the many colorful reef fish that feed along the reef crest, but the sand and seagrass are also full of life. Queen conch are plentiful on the back reef, in addition to hermit crabs, juvenile grunts and snappers, and hundreds of invertebrates. Although the shallow water and sand bottom may tempt you to stand up, please don't, because every bit of the bottom harbors life of some kind.

One of the massive cranes dwarfs a diver over the well deck

steel at frequent intervals. Guide lines made of yellow polypropylene have been installed at various locations, starting at one entryway and bringing you to another. Follow one of these lines and it will bring you in and back out again, but as on any other deep wreck, penetrations should only be attempted by properly trained and equipped divers.

Just cruising the exterior takes a few dives. On the bow, check out the four huge anchor capstans and the forward gun mount, featuring a pair of 3in twin anti-aircraft guns capable of firing 13lb shells over a maximum horizontal range of 7 miles, with a sustained rate of fire of 50 rounds per minute. The barrels were cut off by the navy to render the guns safe when the ship was decommissioned in 1980, but the rest of the emplacement is intact.

Aft of the superstructure, you'll find two more sets of guns, identical to the forward anti-aircraft guns and easily identified by the large recoil springs near the breeches. The gunners' seats, shaped like metal bicycle seats, and the gun controls are still in place. The

The Medallion Program

Accidental capsizing added to the cost of sinking the Spiegel Grove

Sinking the *Spiegel Grove* cost about $1.25 million, much of which was loaned to the community by local banks. The *Spiegel Grove* Medallion Program was implemented as a way to pay back the loans, and to eventually fund other wrecks in the area. Donations of $10 are the heart of the program, and for that you get a medallion to wear on your BCD that entitles you to dive the *Spiegel Grove*, *Bibb*, *Duane* and *Eagle* for a year. The annual medallions can be obtained at any Upper Keys dive shop.

One thousand Lifetime Medallions were also cast for individuals donating $250. In addition to the plastic medallion for the BCD, lifetime donors also receive a gold-finish presentation medallion. The names of the first group of lifetime donors have been inscribed on a plaque that is mounted on the port side of the ship. A second plaque will be added after the remainder of the 1000 lifetime medallions are sold. Some gold medallions are still available at the time of this writing and can be reserved through World Watersports in Key Largo (☎ 800-DIVE-USA), by contacting the Key Largo Chamber of Commerce on ☎ 1-800-822-1088 or by emailing president@keylargochamber.org.

enormous well deck is aft of the guns. Ballast tanks on the ship could be systematically filled to sink this part of the ship until it was half flooded with water, allowing amphibious landing craft to motor straight in and tie up as though they were in a mobile marina.

A pair of industrial-sized cranes rise like a city construction site behind the stacks. The cranes are intact except for the cables, which were coated with grease and were removed prior to the sinking to prevent pollution.

Fish life on the *Spiegel Grove* is amazing. Jewfish, angelfish, parrotfish, surgeonfish, grunts, snapper…the list goes on and on. Swim under the decking that overhangs the forward portion of the well deck and you'll drift into a swirling mass of baitfish.

  13 | BENWOOD

Location: *3.5 nautical miles (6.7km) east southeast of Mosquito Bank light*
Depth Range: *25-45ft (8-14m)*
Access: *Boat*
Expertise Rating: *Novice*

The old tale of a WWII German submarine torpedo attack still does the rounds, but the true nature of this ship's sinking must have been only slightly less terrifying. British-built in 1910, the *Benwood* was 360ft long with a 51ft beam. Her last voyage began on April 6, 1942, when she left Tampa, Florida, for Norfolk, Virginia, loaded with phosphate rock.

The *Benwood* was running without navigation lights, as required at the time due to the possibility of attack by German submarines. The 544ft tanker *Robert C Tuttle* was headed in the opposite direction, also without lights. Unfortunately, both vessels veered off course. In the blackness of 1am on April 9, the

Benwood's bow smashed into the port side of the *Tuttle*. Desperate to save his ship, the *Benwood's* captain attempted to ground the stricken vessel on the reef about six miles south of the **Elbow**. He almost made it, but the ship sank just short of the shallow reefs. After rescuing the crew of the *Benwood,* the *Tuttle* made it safely to port.

Over the years the wreck was used for bombing practice by the military and was intentionally demolished as a hazard to navigation. Now reduced to the crumpled but intact bow section, the bottom of the hull and scattered metal plating, the *Benwood* is one of the fishiest dives in a very fishy sanctuary. Marked by four mooring buoys and one spar buoy, the wreck is about 25ft deep at her stern and 45ft at her bow.

The remaining structures and shallow depth make this an excellent choice for underwater photography, as well as a great night dive. The reds, yellows and purples of the encrusting sponges and corals come alive under the beam of your dive light. Macro photographers will find hundreds of subjects at night on the wreck.

A deeper feature, known as Benwood's Outside Wall, is at about 80ft, although few divers see it because the wreck takes up all their bottom time. More like a terrace, this site is immediately seaward of the *Benwood* and is reached fairly easily from the outer mooring buoy. Chances are good of spotting a turtle or other large animals among the scattered corals here.

Porkfish are common on the wreck of the Benwood

Lots of fish, color and sunlight are trademarks of the Benwood

14 FRENCH REEF

Location: *2 nautical miles (3.8km) northeast of Molasses Reef light*
Depth Range: *12-40ft (4-12m)*
Access: *Boat*
Expertise Rating: *Intermediate*

Old age and perhaps the stress of entertaining so many divers over the decades have taken a toll on French Reef, but it is still an interesting dive. The live coral covering the elaborate ridges that rise 20ft or more off the bottom has gotten thin over the years, leaving a playground of ledges, arches and swim-throughs. It still provides habitat and food for myriads of reef fish, providing lots of company for divers and snorkelers.

Geographical serendipity placed French Reef in a curious position on the reef line. At times, when the overflow of the Gulf Stream is bathing nearby **Molasses Reef** in clear, blue water, French Reef will still be struggling with somewhat murkier green water. After a while the clear blue liquid usually makes it to French, but expect a slightly greener tint to the water here more often than at other reefs.

French Reef encompasses many individual dive sites, including Hourglass Cave, named for its hourglass-shaped supporting pillar, and Christmas Tree Cave, which is topped with a somewhat tree-shaped star coral formation – provided your imagination is limber enough. The latter is about 6ft wide, 4ft high and 15 to 20ft long. Two other caves at French are Sand Bottom Cave, which of course has a smooth, white-sand floor, and Hard Bottom Cave, with a gray fossil coral floor.

None of the arches or caverns at French Reef are difficult to traverse, but care should be taken not to injure marine life on the bottom or overhead as you pass through. Thanks to the reef's designation as a sanctuary preservation area, all common reef fish species are abundant, particularly parrotfish. Stoplight and queen parrotfish nibble the corals singly and in pairs, while midnight parrotfish scavenge in schools of a dozen or more.

15 WHITE BANK

Location: *2 nautical miles (3.8km) north of Molasses Reef light*
Depth Range: *Surface-18ft (6m)*
Access: *Boat*
Expertise Rating: *Novice*

A favorite with snorkel boats, this site is also called White Bank Coral Garden and White Bank Dry Rocks. The site includes two shallow reefs separated by a narrow channel. The reef top is within a few feet of the surface in many spots, and the maximum depth is about 18ft. The northern section of White Bank is composed of one large, dense area of corals with several smaller adjacent patches, while the southern section is made up of smaller clusters. Reef grazers such as butterflyfish and parrotfish are plentiful here, as well as bicolor and yellowtail damselfish.

White Bank is more than a mile closer to shore than **French Reef**, affording it more protection from waves when the wind is up. The trade-off can be limited visibility during windy weather. Green water and 20ft of visibility are about average for the site.

The reef here gets lots of abuse, as it is visited primarily by snorkelers trying the sport for the first time. Too many beginners over the years have swallowed a mouthful of water, panicked and stood up on the coral, but White Bank continues to fascinate because the fish are so prolific.

16 | SAND ISLAND

Location: *0.8 nautical miles (1.5km) northeast of Molasses Reef light*
Depth Range: *12-60ft (4-18m)*
Access: *Boat*
Expertise Rating: *Intermediate*

A small reef next door to mighty **Molasses**, Sand Island is often ignored by divers – which makes it a great destination when **Molasses** is busy. Less than 50 years ago Sand Island actually was an island. The natural forces of wave action and storm surge have removed the sand, leaving a very shallow carpet of coral rubble in the back reef. Amid several small spurs and scattered coral patches are two major coral fingers, neither as high as those on neighboring **Molasses** or **French Reefs**.

The depth at the middle of the three mooring buoys at Sand Island is about 14ft. Swimming seaward, you may discover a large bowl-like depression about 22ft deep, formed by the two main ridges. Hawksbill turtles and nurse sharks often rest on the sand here. From the sand bowl the reef bottom slopes gently down to about 30ft. Scattered sea plumes and sea rods dominate this section of the reef, along with the occasional flattened head of star or brain coral.

Parrotfish are abundant here, especially roving bands of blue parrotfish which munch their way along the reef. They're actually scraping the live polyps and algae from the coral, but they ingest pieces of the reef at the same time. The coral fragments are ground to fine sand in their gullets and excreted back onto the reef. Follow one around for a couple of minutes and you'll see graphic evidence of this process. An active parrotfish can churn out more than 2lbs of sand a day. Groups of six or seven, like the blue parrotfish patrols at Sand Island, can make up to a ton of sand each year.

Hawksbill turtle, Eretmochelys imbriocota

Crocodiles

The Crocodile Lake National Wildlife Refuge sets aside 6686 acres of north Key Largo as a preserve for the endangered American crocodile, *Crocodylus acutus*. The total population is estimated to be between 500 and 1200 crocodiles, but they are rarely observed by visitors to the Keys. If you do chance to see one, the narrow snout and prominent fourth tooth on the lower jaw will confirm that you're looking at a crocodile and not an alligator.

The gregarious sergeant major, found everywhere in the Keys

17 MOLASSES REEF (NORTH)

Location: *4.5 nautical miles (8.6km) southeast of Rodriguez Key*
Depth Range: *10-40ft (3-12m)*
Access: *Boat*
Expertise Rating: *Intermediate*

Along with **Elbow Reef**, Molasses seems to have been blessed in the visibility sweepstakes, enjoying clear blue water more often than most other reefs. And when high winds stir things up and drive the visibility down, Molasses seems to recover quicker.

Depths on this section of Molasses Reef range from 10ft to 40ft, although a determined swim could bring you to much deeper water.

The shallow end of the coral spurs are covered edge to edge with common sea fans and topped with small colonies of elkhorn coral. Pieces of an old tower are scattered across many of the sand channels. The deeper end of the coral spurs is buttressed by exceptionally large star coral mounds. Some of them show the ravages of time, undercut by erosion and invaded by boring sponges; others have an even coat of tiny brown or green polyps and are still going strong.

The real magic of Molasses Reef is the fish life. Even snorkeling at the surface, you'll be face to face with sergeant majors, Bermuda chub, barracuda and yellowtail snappers. In the mid-range, from 20ft to 30ft, Molasses is mobbed by reef fish.

The MV *Wellwood* ran aground on the north end of Molasses Reef in August 1984, grinding a wide swath of the coral into parking-lot smoothness. The ship's owners incurred a settlement of more than $5 million, money that now primarily supports reef restoration efforts. Some of the sanctuary's transplantation efforts are visible on this section of Molasses.

18 MOLASSES REEF (DEEP)

Location: *4.5 nautical miles (8.6km) southeast of Rodriguez Key*
Depth Range: *40-90ft (12-27m)*
Access: *Boat*
Expertise Rating: *Advanced*

The deep reef in front of Molasses is an excellent first dive of the day, providing a profile between about 50ft and 75ft. This is actually part of the transition zone between the shallower spur-and-groove section of Molasses and the sandy plain in deeper water. Vestiges of the spur-and-groove formation are easily observed, but the spurs are lower and the sandy grooves are narrower. Sponges are more plentiful and the hard corals are smaller. The large congregations of snapper, grunts and damselfish that inhabit the main areas of Molasses are not seen here, but there are lots of parrotfish, angelfish and many other species. Chances of encountering larger animals, such as sharks, turtles and rays, are also excellent on this deeper section.

As you head seaward from the mooring pin, the reef slopes gradually downward until you reach the break where a fairly precipitous drop plunges the reef down to the sandy flat. If there is a current present, as is often the case, it may be stronger along this break than in shallower water.

The deep reef on Molasses is frequently dived as a drift dive, which eliminates the need for navigation. If your boat is tied up to a mooring though, it can be trickier to find your way back in this area because the landmarks are less obvious. Keeping track of the coral ridges and sand gullies will help. It's also a good idea to take a depth reading at the base of the mooring before you head off on your dive, so you can limit your search to the right depth contour when you return.

Hawksbill turtle encounters occur quite often

Mixed schooling: goatfish and grunts

19 MOLASSES REEF (SOUTH)

Location: *4.5 nautical miles (8.6km) southeast of Rodriguez Key*
Depth Range: *10-40ft (3-12m)*
Access: *Boat*
Expertise Rating: *Intermediate*

1887 winch left on Molasses Reef

The south end of Molasses Reef must rank among the top 10 most visited coral reefs in the world, with a constant procession of dive and snorkel boats coming and going from Key Largo. There's good reason for the reef's popularity too, because Molasses rarely disappoints. Whether you dive or snorkel, you're bound to see something here to make the trip worthwhile.

The southernmost buoy marks Permit Ledge, a long coral and sponge-covered ledge facing sand flats and a low hard bottom. Divers here often encounter large animals, including permits, spotted eagle rays and nurse sharks. Cross the flats south of Permit Ledge and you'll come to another ledge, this one topped with five or six colonies of pillar coral.

Slightly to the north is a site called Fire Coral Caves, where a deeply undercut coral ledge harbors Atlantic spadefish, dog snappers and schoolmasters. A large jewfish sometimes hovers beneath the ledge, and half a dozen permits frequently hang about the area. Some fire coral grows atop the ridge, but the reddish hue in the caves is due to the encrusting corals and sponges.

The Spanish Anchor is a bit northeast of Fire Coral Caves, lying flat on the bottom. Further to the north is the Winch Hole, where a large coral-encrusted windlass is all that remains of the sailing ship *Slobodna* that ran aground on Molasses in 1887. Along the coral ridge, Hole in the Wall is a split that leads into an oval chamber.

When a current is running at Molasses Reef, it's usually strongest at the south end. Watch the way the water flows past your boat after you are mooring, and use caution if you detect a strong current.

20 THREE SISTERS

Location: *3 nautical miles (5.7km) east southeast of Rodriguez Key*
Depth Range: *10-20ft (3-6m)*
Access: *Boat*
Expertise Rating: *Novice*

Only one of the 'three sisters' survives today, so you'll have to imagine a line of three green markers if you want to understand the origin of this dive site name. A trio of navigation aids used

Flamingo tongue nibbling its way along a sea fan

to mark a shipping channel running past here from **Molasses Reef** to Hawk Channel. Since large vessels haven't passed that way in some time, the Coast Guard elected not to replace the markers as they fell into disrepair. When the remaining marker goes, the name will really be a mystery.

Three Sisters is a series of shallow patch reefs. The largest is to the northwest of the site, while a string of smaller reefs trails off to the southeast. Depths range from 10ft on the flat dome of the reef top to 18ft or 20ft on the surrounding sand. The reefs to the southeast are close enough together that you can swim from one to the other if your underwater navigation is reasonably proficient.

Used frequently by fishermen, Three Sisters is usually overlooked by divers unless the weather kicks up. Regardless of the weather, though, it's a nice site to snorkel or just poke around on scuba. Macro-photography here is excellent, with numerous subjects just the right size for macro tubes or a close-up lens. Look for common invertebrates such as Christmas tree worms, arrow crabs, flamingo tongues and painted tunicates, as well as many juvenile fish.

Bibb, the sideways Coast Guard Cutter

21 BIBB

Location: *1 nautical mile (1.9km) south southeast of Molasses Reef light*
Depth Range: *100-130ft (30-40m)*
Access: *Boat*
Expertise Rating: *Advanced*

Launched in 1936 and named for former US Secretary of the Treasury George Motier Bibb, the *Bibb* was a 327ft US Coast Guard cutter with a 41ft beam. She was powered by twin Westinghouse steam turbines and put her 7000 range to good use during WWII, serving in the Atlantic, Caribbean, Mediterranean and Pacific. On convoy escort duty in 1943, the *Bibb* saved 202 people when the troop ship SS *Henry Mallory* was torpedoed by the German submarine *U-402*. *Bibb* crew members actually jumped into the frigid water to rescue the nearly frozen survivors. That same night the *Bibb* also rescued 33 sailors from the torpedoed freighter SS *Kalliopi*. Later in the war, she was reassigned to the Pacific, taking part in the battle for Okinawa in 1945. The *Bibb* also served in Vietnam in 1968 and '69. Decommissioned in 1985, the *Bibb* was languishing under a foot

dive operators will only take advanced divers with recent experience to the *Bibb* and do not permit penetrations.

The *Bibb's* position on the bottom has made a difference in the accumulation of coral and sponges. The thick coat of colorful cup corals and bright encrusting sponges that decorate the *Duane* has not appeared on the *Bibb,* at least not to the same spectacular degree. Although a dive light will bring out some nice pinks and reds, the *Bibb* is a bit drab compared to the *Duane.*

Does this mean the *Bibb* isn't a good dive? Not at all! This wreck is packed with fish and the intact structure offers plenty of scenic stops. The props are nearly always surrounded by jacks and barracuda. The crow's-nest on the aftermast is thick with growth and hangs neatly out over the sand. The huge anchor windlass is pink with encrusted growth, along with the thick anchor chains.

Bibb, the sideways Coast Guard Cutter

of snow in a Boston shipyard when she was chosen for this final mission.

The *Bibb* is the *Duane's* unlucky sister, having landed on her starboard side when she was intentionally sunk as a dive site back in 1987. That unfortunate circumstance means that the *Bibb* is a significantly deeper dive. The shallowest structure is the port side of the hull, which you won't reach until you've descended about 100ft. Although the ship was prepped for diver penetrations above the main deck, incursions into the vessel should only be undertaken by experienced and properly equipped dive teams due to the sideways orientation and depth. Most Key Largo

The Bibb can be one of the 'sharkiest' dives in the Keys, too. Divers often see bull and reef sharks cruising the wreck and nurse sharks are frequently spotted lying in the sand with their noses up against the hull. A pair of Jewfish that outweigh most sharks greet nearly every diver that ventures past the pilothouse.

Nearly all of your dive will be below 100ft and it's a long way back to the surface, so don't push your dive computer to the no deco limit, and start up early.

22	DUANE

Location: *1.2 nautical miles (2.3km) south southeast of Molasses Reef light*
Depth Range: *50-115ft (15-35m)*
Access: *Boat*
Expertise Rating: *Advanced*

The *Duane* has aged beautifully, donning a gorgeous cloak of orange cup coral and applying bright sponges to her plain steel sides. This is one of the most colorful wrecks anywhere, and one of the most densely populated. You'll probably meet the barracudas first, a permanent squadron of them act as sentinels patrolling the upper reaches of the mast. The barracudas share their space with fast swimming mobs of predatory jacks, including some big amberjacks that are not at all reticent about approaching divers. The wreck itself is home to thousands of reef fish. Bring along a waterproof fish guide if you want to sort them all out.

Like her sister ship the *Bibb*, the *Duane* is named for a former Treasury Secretary, in this case William John Duane, Secretary of the Treasury under President Andrew Jackson. She was built in Pennsylvania in 1936 at the Philadelphia Navy Yard for just under $2.5 mil-

lion. When you consider that it would cost about that much to sink a similar ship as a dive site now, the *Duane's* construction was quite a bargain.

Twin steam turbines generated 6200HP, which was applied via a pair of 9ft three-bladed props, giving the *Duane* an 11 knot cruise speed and a 20.5 knot maximum speed. Armament consisted of one 5in gun initially, but was increased during WWII.

The *Duane* served as a convoy escort in the north Atlantic during the early part of the war. In 1942, she rescued 229 people when the troop-carrying passenger ship SS *Dorchester* was torpedoed by the German submarine *U-233*. In the following year, she and another Coast Guard Cutter called the *Spencer* forced the German submarine *U-175* to the surface with depth charges and took 22 of the sub's crew prisoner. At Normandy, the *Duane* had the honor to be chosen as the flagship of Maj Gen John O'Daniel during the invasion of France. After WWII, the ship returned to normal duty patrolling the US coast and saving many lives. Between 1957 and

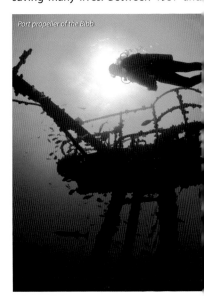
Port propeller of the Bibb

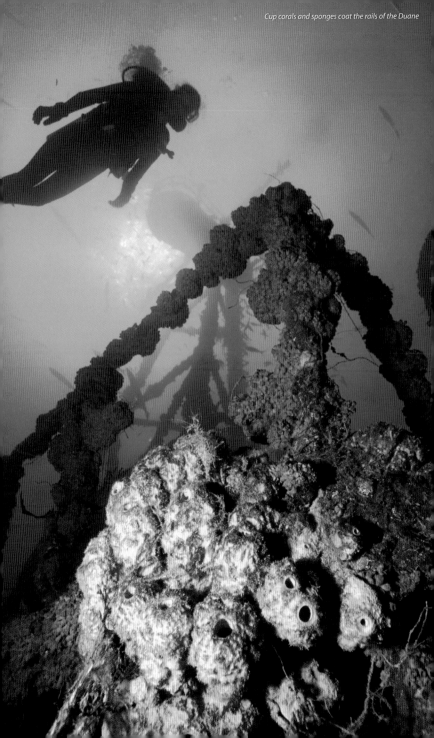
Cup corals and sponges coat the rails of the Duane

The Duane is ablaze in color, thanks to a thick coating of coral and sponge

1968 she returned to war as part of the Coastal Surveillance Force in Vietnam. Ironically, in 1980 the cutter actually steamed over the spot where she now rests, on the way to Key West for escort duty during the massive Mariel Boatlift, which brought nearly 125,000 Cuban refugees to the Florida Keys.

All weapons were removed when the ship was decommissioned in 1985, but the mounts are still visible. The *Duane* was sunk on November 27, 1987, by the Key Largo Artificial Reef Association in conjunction with various state, county and federal programs, as well as numerous local businesses and individuals.

Although the *Duane* is upright, she is still in deep water frequently swept by strong currents and is considered an advanced dive by all local dive shops.

Most of the superstructure is easily accessed, but use caution – air and bottom time can be used up more quickly than you realize while you're exploring the wreck.

23　PILLAR CORAL PATCH

Location: *4 nautical miles (7.6km) southeast of Rodriguez Key*
Depth Range: *15-30ft (4-9m)*
Access: *Boat*
Expertise Rating: *Intermediate*

Two moorings mark this small but delightful site just north of **Pickles Reef**. On a coral ridge next to a prominent

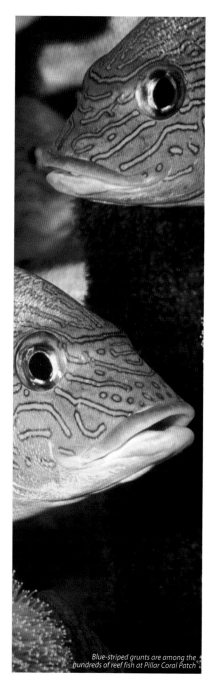

sand channel, you'll find a cluster of more than two-dozen pillar coral colonies. In surprisingly pristine condition, considering the number of severe storms the area has suffered during the last couple of years, the pillar corals have the castle-like appearance of an underwater theme park. Please use extreme caution swimming through the area, to avoid being the cause of any damage to the fragile formations.

As you might expect, the pillars are home to hundreds of reef fish. Grunts, especially bluestriped, small mouth and French grunts, account for most of the constantly moving mass, but there are lots of squirrelfish, rock beauties, margates, trumpetfish and porkfish in the mix too. Even the big guys are present and a watchful eye may catch sight of a

Blue-striped grunts are among the hundreds of reef fish at Pillar Coral Patch

big green moray or a large jewfish. Nassau and black grouper skirt around the fringes as well.

A determined pair of divers can reach deep water from nearly any of the outer reef location in the Keys, and Pillar Coral Patch is no exception. Be prepared for a long swim though. A better plan is to hover quietly over the sand channel next to the pillar coral and let the fish get used to your presence. In five minutes you'll be surrounded by fish.

24 PICKLES

Location: *4 nautical miles (7.6km) southeast of Rodriguez Key*
Depth Range: *10-80ft (3-24m)*
Access: *Boat*
Expertise Rating: *Intermediate*

Common sea fans cover the crest of Pickles so thickly it looks like a sea fan farm. It's a fascinating area to snorkel, with the sea fans waving gently in the surge like a wheat field in the morning breeze. With lots of fish and nicely scattered hard corals, the shallows of Pickles are an excellent choice for snorkelers.

The 19th century wreck that gives this reef its name also lies in these shallows, in about 10ft of water near the two metal stakes that mark the reef crest. The Pickle Barrel Wreck was actually an early exercise in recycling, since the pickle barrels were not filled with pickles but with mortar, possibly for the construction of Fort Jefferson in the Dry Tortugas. The wood of the barrels is long gone, but the mortar mixed with seawater and formed concrete, leaving a number of barrel-shaped concrete plugs on the bottom.

The sides of the vessel are surprisingly intact for such an exposed wreck and shelter many juvenile fish and invertebrates.

Pillar coral, though easily damaged by divers, is surprisingly robust in strong surge

Depth at the mooring buoys is about 15ft. A short snorkel toward land will take you along the reef crest; if you head seaward on scuba, you'll descend a gradual slope to 70ft or 80ft before the reef peters out.

The highlights of the reef are close to the buoys, so a long swim is not required. Several wedge-shaped sand channels run past the buoys. The sides are formed by 5ft-high coral ledges that are undercut 2ft to 3ft. During the day hundreds of grunts and snappers line the ledges. Several large, healthy colonies of star, starlet and brain corals sit in isolation on the sand.

When you first enter the water, look carefully around at the limits of your vision. Turtles and nurse sharks often shelter along the margins of the sand channels and can be closely approached if you are patient and careful.

An ancient star coral colony plays host to many other organisms, including this large sea fan

French angelfish join a variety of grunts beneath elkhorn coral

Plantation & Upper Matecumbe Keys

0 — 3 km
0 — 2 miles
not for navigation

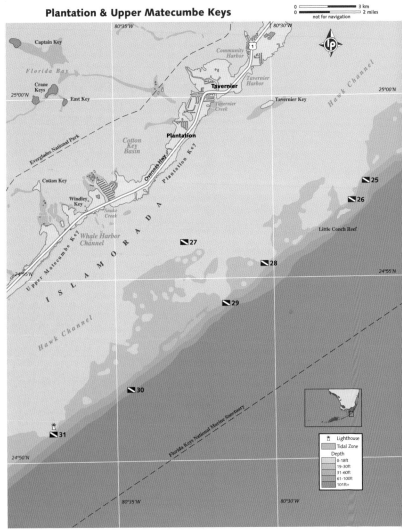

Captain Key

Florida Bay

80°35'W   80°30'W

Community Harbor   1

Crane Keys

East Key

Tavernier

Tavernier Harbor

25°00'N   25°00'N

Tavernier Key

Tavernier Creek

Hawk Channel

Everglades National Park

Cotton Key Basin

Plantation

Cotton Key

Overseas Hwy

Plantation Key

Windley Key

Snake Creek

25

26

Little Conch Reef

Whale Harbor Channel

27

I S L A M O R A D A

28

24°55'N   24°55'N

Upper Matecumbe Key

29

Hawk Channel

30

31

Florida Keys National Marine Sanctuary

24°50'N

Lighthouse
Tidal Zone
Depth
0-18ft
19-30ft
31-60ft
61-100ft
101ft+

80°35'W   80°30'W

72

Plantation & Upper Matecumbe Keys

25 **CONCH WALL**

Location: *3.5 nautical miles (6.7km) southeast of Tavernier Key*
Depth Range: *60-90ft (18-27m)*
Access: *Boat*
Expertise Rating: *Advanced*

Helmet conch

Conch Wall is one of the few places in the Florida Keys where the reef forms anything resembling a vertical wall. Dropping steeply from 60ft to 90ft, this is also one of the deepest sections of living reef. The wall is festooned with deep-water sea fans and several species of barrel sponges, including giant, leathery and green barrel sponges. You'll see lots of red and purple finger sponges, too.

Angelfish, parrotfish, wrasses and other reef fish are plentiful along the wall, but it's the possibility of seeing larger animals that brings divers here time after time. Big jacks, like the speedy crevalle jacks, are nearly always around. Greater amberjacks and permits show up from time to time, while you'll likely spot several species of grouper, including black, Nassau and yellowfin groupers. Jewfish have come back to the site in recent years too.

Keep an occasional eye out toward the deep water, because bull sharks, hammerheads, spotted eagle rays and even mantas have been known to cruise silently by. They seem to be attracted by divers, but stay back almost out of sight.

Drift dive Conch Wall when a current is running – which is most of the time – and you'll feel like you're flying. Choosing your entry point and timing your descent can be tricky, but then you can relax and go with the flow. Towards the end of your dive, you can either ascend directly to a safety stop or head up any one of the sand chutes leading to shallower water atop **Conch Reef**.

Key Largo & the Upper Keys

	GOOD SNORKELING	NOVICE	INTERMEDIATE	ADVANCED
25 CONCH WALL				•
26 CONCH REEF	•		•	
27 HEN & CHICKENS	•	•		
28 DAVIS REEF	•	•		
29 CROCKER REEF				•
30 EAGLE				•
31 ALLIGATOR REEF				•

Mooring Buoys

The coral reef-friendly mooring system utilizing embedded anchors in place of heavy weights or chains was developed by the National Marine Sanctuary program in the Florida Keys. More than 200 buoys have been installed in the Keys, nearly eliminating the need to anchor.

Using the first-come, first-served buoys couldn't be easier. Approach the buoy from downwind (or down-current), use a boat hook to retrieve the floating yellow pick-up line and secure your boat to the eye spliced in the end. This is easiest if you tie one of your dock lines to a bow cleat first, then pick up the mooring line. Pass the free end of your dock line through the pick-up line eye and secure it to another cleat or on top of the first one. You should be left with a line that loops from your boat through the eye of the pick-up line and back. Simply reverse the procedure to let go of the mooring.

26 CONCH REEF

Location: *3.5 nautical miles (6.7km) southeast of Tavernier Key*
Depth Range: *18-60ft (6-18m)*
Access: *Boat*
Expertise Rating: *Intermediate*

Early settlers used to walk into the shallows and pick up conch without even getting their elbows wet. In fact, people ate conch so often they came to be called 'Conchs' themselves, and the name still applies to lifetime residents of the Keys. Over-harvesting nearly wiped out queen conch, but they have been protected for many years and are regaining their former numbers at sites throughout the Keys. They're not common on the fore reef, but put on a snorkel and check out the sand flats and seagrass behind the reef crest. You'll see quite a lot of them grazing in the grass in about 20ft of water.

Conch Reef is the current home of the Aquarius undersea research center. Free public access would interrupt many of the research projects underway at Aquarius, so the area around the underwater lab is marked off with yellow buoys and restricted to those with sanctuary research permits. Resist the temptation to see what's going on, otherwise you may find the sanctuary patrol waiting when you return to your boat.

The reef outside the research zone has plenty to offer. Conch Reef is slightly deeper than neighboring reefs, so it's thick with gorgonians and barrel sponges, lending the topography a lush fullness. Look beyond the waving sea plumes and sea rods though, and you'll also find many medium-sized star and boulder brain corals. Snappers and hogfish are particularly plentiful on Conch Reef. Hog snappers like to cruise among the gorgonians as they feed, and schoolmasters gather in small schools near the ledges.

Use caution when surfacing, as Conch Reef is one of the few Sanctuary Preservation Areas that allow trolling for fish by boat.

Honeycomb cowfish, Lactophrys polygonia

27 HEN & CHICKENS

Location: *2 nautical miles (3.8km) east southeast of Snake Creek*
Depth Range: *5-20ft (2-6m)*
Access: *Boat*
Expertise Rating: *Novice*

Marked by a lighted tower, Hen and Chickens is a popular spot for three reasons. The first is its convenient location, less than 2 nautical miles from shore,

almost in the middle of Hawk Channel. The second is that it's protected from rough seas. When high winds bring waves to the outer reefs, Hen and Chickens experiences a comfortable chop. When the seas are calm, Hen and Chickens is like a swimming pool with a living bottom. The third reason is that the reef structure itself is fascinating. The combination of these factors led to the designation of this reef as a Sanctuary Preservation Area. The accompanying ban on fishing has only made the diving better.

The site comprises a series of enormous mounds of hard-coral colonies, principally star and brain corals. These are mature colonies, several hundred years old, and are starting to show their age. In addition to the boulder hard corals, Hen and Chickens supports many species of sponge and soft coral, which give the reef a lush appearance.

The downside of Hen and Chickens' mid-channel position is the possibility of limited visibility. Generally the reef is bathed in green water, and any surge tends to stir up sediments from the bottom. Moderate currents may be experienced during peak tidal flow. Visibility of 20ft to 30ft is a worthwhile trade-off, though, when the weather keeps you off the main reefs, and of course there are numerous days when even Hen and Chickens sparkles in clear water.

Gulf Stream

As coral reefs go, the reefs of the Florida Keys are located well north of the usual growth pattern, and we have the Gulf Stream to thank. Hundreds of times larger than the Mississippi River, the Gulf Stream flows by the Keys and up the Florida coast with clear, warm water that is perfect for growing coral. Enough of that water filters through the Keys to support this magnificent reef system.

Caesar grunts, Haemulon carbonarium

28 DAVIS REEF

Location: *4 nautical miles (7.6km) south of Tavernier Key*
Depth Range: *15-30ft (5-9m)*
Access: *Boat*
Expertise Rating: *Novice*

The bottom structure at Davis Reef is very different from other nearby reefs. The main part of the reef consists of a long coral ledge running generally north-south. Landward of the ledge is a long sand flat, speckled with soft-ball-sized hard corals and diminutive sea plumes. The ledge rises 4ft or 5ft above the sand and is undercut deeply in places. Orange elephant ear sponges encrust the underside and face of the ledge, and hundreds of Caesar grunts, schoolmasters and bluestriped grunts shelter cheek to cheek in the shadow of the ledge.

If you cross perpendicular to the ledge and swim seaward, you'll pass over a fairly uniform hard bottom with some scattered hard corals, including several large and healthy starlet and brain corals toward the north end of the reef. Most of these isolated coral mounds are

cleaning stations, where juvenile Spanish hogfish and neon gobies eat the ectoparasites off bar jacks, parrotfish and other customers. After 150ft to 200ft the hard bottom peters out, giving way to a vast sandy plain covered with large sea plumes and dozens of black loggerhead sponges.

A 2ft bronze statue of a seated Buddha was placed in the sand at the south end of Davis Reef in 1989. Before it was stolen by vandals a few years ago, the Buddha's head and belly were highly polished from the hands of divers who rubbed the statue for good luck. Another smaller Buddha has now been set in its place.

29 CROCKER REEF

Location: *4 nautical miles (7.6km) southeast of Snake Creek*
Depth Range: *17-90ft (5-27m)*
Access: *Boat*
Expertise Rating: *Intermediate*

Two moorings are in place at Crocker; one in about 55ft and one in 40ft. Starting a dive from the shallower buoy, you'll find low-profile coral fingers topped with medium-sized star coral heads, as well as a few convoluted and smooth brain corals. Giant barrel, leathery barrel and brown tube sponges grow in large numbers on the fingers, along with many sea fans and sea plumes. The fingers are not continuous here, and run toward deeper water in a broken pattern that may be difficult to follow. The sand channels are generally quite narrow, but open up occasionally, creating spacious sand pockets. A sizeable population of yellowhead jawfish lives in these pockets, hovering vertically over their holes as they pluck bits of food from the water. Blue angelfish are also common on this section of Crocker Reef, as are rock beauties and honeycomb cowfish.

A long swim to seaward will take you down a very gentle slope until you finally reach the shelf break at 60ft. The reef drops away steeply here, then levels out on a sandy plain at about 90ft. A current may be present anytime on Crocker, but you'll frequently experience

A queen angelfish nibbles on a sponge snack

a significant flow along the shelf break. The edge of the shelf is an active zone, with big schools of bluestriped grunts, schoolmasters and Creole wrasses hugging the coral on top.

If you head toward shallower water from the moorings, you eventually come to a hard bottom reef crest in about 17ft. Scattered plate-sized heads of hard coral and many soft corals dot the area, along with considerable coral rubble. Blue tangs, yellowtail snappers and a variety of damselfish are among the reef fish common in this shallow area.

Crocker is not a Sanctuary Preservation Area, but it is well marked by the number 16 red nun, so expect heavy fishing boat traffic, especially on the weekends.

| 30 | **EAGLE** |

Location: *3 nautical miles (5.7km) northeast of Alligator Reef light*
Depth Range: *80-110 ft (24-37m)*
Access: *Boat*
Expertise Rating: *Advanced*

This 269ft freighter became the MV *Eagle* in acknowledgement of the Eagle Tire Company's financial support in the effort to sink her as an artificial reef. Launched in Holland in 1962, she was powered by a 10-cylinder diesel engine, and capable of cruising at 12.5 knots. During the next two decades she sailed under a variety of names, including *Raila Dan, Barok, Carmela, Ytai, Etai, Carigulf Pioneer* and *Aaron K*, and it was while she was known under the last of these names that disaster struck. She was transporting newspaper and cardboard from the US to Central and South America when a serious fire broke out while the ship was en route from Miami to Venezuela in 1985. Much of

the electrical system and machinery of the vessel was damaged beyond repair by the fire, and the ship was declared a total loss by the insurers and towed to Miami.

Members of the Islamorada diving community, looking for a suitable ship to sink, found her there and made the arrangements to have the ship cleaned and towed to the Keys. The day before the sinking, the ship broke free and drifted a short distance before an anchor could be dropped. The following day – December 19, 1985 – high explosives were used to blow holes in the hull, sinking the ship in less than two minutes. Unfortunately, the *Eagle* settled on her starboard side, giving the ship a deeper profile than intended. The ship is a great deep dive, though, with lots of coral-encrusted rigging, including the crow's-nest and two masts. Depth to the port rail is about 80ft, and the bottom is about 110ft.

In 1998 the powerful storm surge of Hurricane Georges broke the hull in two, leaving a V-shaped gap amidships

Atlantic spadefish call the Eagle home

Powerful blasts opened the bottom of the Eagle on December 19, 1985

and opening sections of the interior that were previously inaccessible. The broken hull has proven remarkably stable since then, but both sections of the ship are gradually settling into the sand. The propeller that was originally hanging in mid-water is now half buried and the rudder has fallen off. Penetration of the wreck should only be attempted by trained divers with proper equipment because of the depth, sideways orientation and damage from the explosives and storms. Guided penetrations are available from several local shops.

Don't neglect the hull side if you have time – it's a garden of hard and soft corals with lots of encrusting sponges thrown in for color. There are even a few fuzzy black coral colonies growing back there. The huge holes from the explosives can be seen too, but take care because the metal edges are still jagged after all these years.

The *Eagle* always hosts an entertaining cadre of guests, including tarpon, barracuda, Atlantic spadefish and dozens of species of reef fish. Several turtles and three big Jewfish seem to have taken up permanent residence as well.

31 ALLIGATOR REEF

Location: *5 nautical miles (9.5km) south of Whale Harbor Channel*
Depth Range: *10-50ft (3-15m)*
Access: *Boat*
Expertise Rating: *Intermediate*

This reef was originally called Carysford Reef, but was renamed Alligator Reef for the ship that was lost here on November 9, 1822. The USS *Alligator*, an 86ft, 12-cannon schooner, was constructed in Boston in 1820 for the US Navy to combat slavery and piracy. After a few initial successes, the ship unfortunately ran aground on this reef and was blown up by the crew to keep it from falling into the hands of pirates.

A lighthouse was scheduled to be built on Alligator Reef in 1857, but construction was delayed because of the Civil War. The existing lighthouse was finally completed in 1873. Manned until 1963, this historic structure is 136ft high and is still in operation, using an automated system. The buoy closest to the lighthouse marks the spot where two piles of ballast stones and bits of the lower hull of the Alligator wreckage lie in about 10ft of water. The four buoys southeast of the lighthouse are aligned along the edge of the main reef.

Spiny lobsters come warily out of their holes

The coral ridges at Alligator are somewhat flattened, forming an extensive system of low but deeply undercut ledges lined with encrusting sponges and corals. These ledges support a variety of invertebrates, including arrow crabs, spiny lobsters and Spanish lobsters. Caesar and French grunts are abundant, schooling atop the ledges or sheltering in their lee when a current is running. Depths here range from about 20ft on the back reef to 50ft on the seaward side.

Use caution when surfacing, as Alligator Reef is one of the few Sanctuary Preservation Areas that allow trolling for fish by boat.

French grunt (Haemulon flavolineatum)

A spiny lobster sheltering beneath a sponge.

Middle Keys

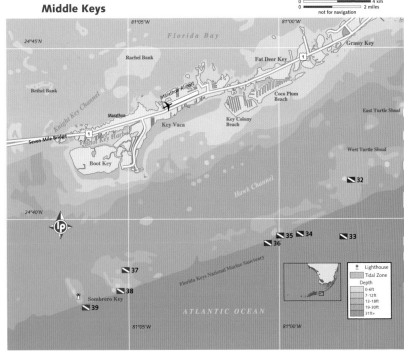

0 ⎯⎯⎯⎯⎯⎯ 4 km
0 ⎯⎯⎯⎯⎯⎯ 2 miles
not for navigation

24°45'N

81°05'W   81°00'W

Florida Bay

Grassy Key

Rachel Bank   Fat Deer Key

Bethel Bank

Knight Key Channel   Marathon Airport   Coco Plum Beach   East Turtle Shoal

Marathon

Seven Mile Bridge   Key Vaca   Key Colony Beach   West Turtle Shoal

Boot Key Harbor

Boot Key

Hawk Channel

☠32

24°40'N

☠35 ☠34

☠36   ☠33

☠37

Florida Keys National Marine Sanctuary

☠38

Sombrero Key

☠39

ATLANTIC OCEAN

	Lighthouse
	Tidal Zone
Depth	
	0-6ft
	7-12ft
	13-18ft
	19-30ft
	31ft+

81°05'W   81°00'W

Marathon & the Middle Keys

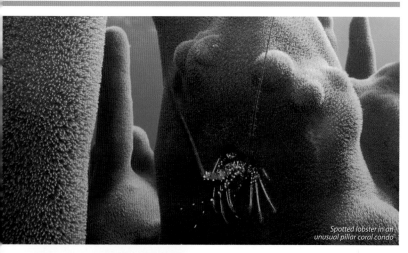

Spotted lobster in an unusual pillar coral condo

32 COFFINS PATCH

Location: *4 nautical miles (7.6km) southeast of Key Colony Beach*
Depth Range: *15-25ft (5-8m)*
Access: *Boat*
Expertise Rating: *Novice*

This reef was labeled 'Coffin's Patches' on early marine charts, suggesting it may have been named after a person, though stories circulate of a ship that ran aground here while carrying a load of coffins. The reef is on the long sand bank that runs seaward of Hawk Channel, with flat, irregularly shaped mounds of coral enclosing scattered sand pockets. The shallow depths of Coffins Patch make it a favorite second dive.

Southern stingrays often rest or feed atop the sand at Coffins Patch. If you hang back a few minutes to acclimate the ray to your presence, it may let you approach very closely. Rays feed primarily on mollusks and other invertebrates

buried in the sand. They locate their prey with finely tuned senses then suck the hapless victims out of the sand. Their blunt jaws with fused teeth are hard enough to crush armored carapaces and even heavy shells. Watch one feed and you'll see the sand being vented out through their gill slits.

The west end of the reef features extensive pillar coral formations. Most hard corals rely on the symbiotic algae within their tissues for energy during the day and keep their polyps retracted until night-time. Pillar coral polyps,

Marathon & the Middle Keys	GOOD SNORKELING	NOVICE	INTERMEDIATE	ADVANCED
32 COFFINS PATCH	•	•		
33 THUNDERBOLT				•
34 THE GAP				•
35 SAMANTHA'S REEF	•	•		
36 HERMAN'S HOLE	•	•		
37 FLAGLER'S BARGE	•	•		
38 DELTA SHOAL	•	•		
39 SOMBRERO REEF			•	

83

however, feed actively in daylight, and their extended tentacles give this coral a fuzzy appearance. Daytime feeding habits and slender skeletal pillars make this coral very susceptible to damage from divers, so use caution when swimming nearby.

As on most of the inshore reefs, visibility is highly variable at Coffins Patch. Most of the time it will be around 30ft, but it can be as high as 50ft or 60ft, or as low as 10ft or 15ft. If you arrive when visibility is down, don't fret. The reef is always packed with life – just narrow your focus and enjoy the show.

33 THUNDERBOLT

Location: *2.5 nautical miles (4.7km) south of West Turtle Shoal*
Depth Range: *75-120 ft (23-37m)*
Access: *Boat*
Expertise Rating: *Advanced*

Originally designed as a coastal mine-layer, the *Thunderbolt* was built in 1942 for the US Army.

With an overall length of 188ft, she was similar in design to another Army minelayer that ended up on the bot-tom in the Florida Keys, the *Cayman Salvage Master*. The *Thunderbolt* was transferred to the Navy in 1949, then acquired by a commercial company in 1961 for use as a cable layer. The huge open-spoked cable wheel is still mounted on the forward deck, and is one of the wreck's most recognizable features. *Thunderbolt's* name, though, came after she was retired by the military and purchased by Florida Power & Light for research into lightning strikes. A turbine engine mounted on the aft deck churned out lightning-at-tracting ions as the ship plowed through coastal storms. It's difficult to imagine what the crew must have been thinking as they waiting for the big zap to hit.

The ship was set to begin another career, this time in underwater survey-ing, when she sank while docked on the Miami River. The dive operators and businesses in Marathon collected money to have *Thunderbolt* cleaned and towed to the Keys, where she was qui-etly scuttled on March 3, 1986.

The top of the superstructure is now about 75ft deep. The cable wheel is at about 85ft. The entire ship, including wheelhouse and lower crew's quarters is open to diver access. The engine compartments are also wide open, al-lowing easy entry into the deepest part

Underwater Navigation

Finding your way underwater can be tricky, no matter where you dive. Many Florida Keys reefs feature a structure that can help. It's called 'spur-and-groove,' and refers to the way coral grows on the main reefs. Hold your hand out, fingers spread and palm facing away. That's the way the reef looks. Your fingers are the coral ridges, the space between them the sandy channels. The water gets deeper toward your fingertips and shallower toward your palm.

The ridges may be tall and easy to follow in some places and barely discernable in oth-ers, but they always run the same way. Follow them and you'll either be getting deeper or shallower. Cross them and you'll stay at the same depth. You can even keep count as you cross them, to keep track of how far you have to come back.

Naturally, an underwater compass is always useful. Practice the proper techniques for using a compass before your dive trip, so you'll be able to navigate easily when you arrive.

Encrusted cable reel on the bow of the Thunderbolt

of the ship. The aft deck and the sides of the hull are coated with gorgonians, small hard coral colonies and encrusting sponges that provide some nice color. The depth on the bottom next to the partially exposed twin screws is about 120ft. If you look carefully, welded letters on the ship's stern reveal her original name to be USS *Randolph*.

Gloves aren't recommended in most of the national marine sanctuary, but strong currents are common here, and you may need gloves to protect your hands from fire coral and hydroids on the mooring line during the descent and ascent.

34   THE GAP

Location: *4 nautical miles (7.6km) south southeast of Key Colony Beach*
Depth Range: *50-80ft (15-24m)*
Access: *Boat*
Expertise Rating: *Advanced*

Two nautical miles southwest of **Coffins Patch**, the Gap is a wide cut on the edge of the reef shelf. The depth atop the cut is about 50ft. From the reef top, the bottom slopes steeply downward,

Star coral heads, old enough to be your great, great, great grandfather!

35 SAMANTHA'S REEF

Location: *3.5 nautical miles (6.7km) south of Key Colony Beach*
Depth Range: *15-35ft (5-11m)*
Access: *Boat*
Expertise Rating: *Novice*

A long, winding ledge with deeply undercut sides is the defining feature of Samantha's Reef. The depth is about 15ft atop the ledge and 25ft at the large oval sand patch in the middle of the reef. Heading south, you'll gradually reach water 30ft to 35ft deep, but your best bet is to move east and west, following the main ledge and exploring the nearby smaller ones. Medium-sized colonies of smooth and grooved brain corals and smooth globes of starlet coral are scattered along the upper surfaces of the ledges, along with an assortment of soft corals and tube sponges. Cracks bisect the ledges, opening narrow gaps that shelter numerous squirrelfish and blackbar soldierfish.

The fish are very active at Samatha's, streaming constantly along the ledges like commuters going to work. Smallmouth grunts, surgeonfish and yellowtail snappers gather in mixed groups, then parade off to their next stop on the reef. Schools of gray Bermuda chub are also abundant here, swimming more aggressively above the coral.

The nurse sharks at Samatha's are unfazed by divers, having been fed by local dive operators for years. In fact, the site is called Samatha's ledge after a particularly gregarious nurse shark. Enjoy the encounters or make the most of the photo op, but keep your hands and fingers tucked away so they aren't mistaken for food. A number of exceptionally large and equally pushy southern stingrays are also drawn here by the feeding activity.

terminating in a flat sand bottom 75ft to 80ft deep. Not quite a wall, but interestingly steep. You may encounter strong currents at this site, especially in this deep section. The coral cover is thickest close to the edge of the drop-off, thinning into isolated patches on the sand.

Several species of reef fish frequently congregate in schools and loose packs along the top of the Gap, including bar jacks, schoolmasters and Creole wrasses. French angelfish, rock beauties and other angelfish species are nearly always present, staying close to the coral along the slope and nibbling on the sponges. Green barrel sponges and deepwater sea fans stand among the sea plumes and giant star corals scattered along the slope face.

The boundary between the bottom of the slope and the sand flats is a corridor of sorts for pelagic animals. It's worth investing a few minutes of your bottom time here, in case any jacks, rays or sharks come cruising past.

Juvenile striped parrotfish swarm over the reef

36 HERMAN'S HOLE

Location: *3.5 nautical miles (6.7km) south of Key Colony Beach*
Depth Range: *15-30ft (5-9m)*
Access: *Boat*
Expertise Rating: *Novice*

A large, sandy hole marks the center of Herman's Hole. Depths here range from 15ft to 30ft, and the reef top features a nice balance of hard corals, gorgonians and sponges.

Some of the common sea fans are huge, and there are several unblemished spheres of smooth brain coral. Branching vase sponges are abundant, and you'll see lots of orange encrusting sponges if you peer down into the cracks that split the reef top occasionally.

Two species of rays often rest or feed in the circular sand pockets – large gray southern stingrays and smaller, yellow-and-black yellow stingrays. Nurse sharks sometimes rest on the sand, too, usually around the margin of the pocket or in the many smaller sand channels on the reef.

A long ledge forms the northern edge of the reef, its face undercut and split by numerous small ravines. Everyone sees the squirrelfish, bluestriped grunts and porkfish that gather here, but too many divers hurry along the ledge like it's a highway with a minimum speed limit. The diversity of marine life that finds shelter here is amazing. Cut your throttles back to idle and you'll find fascinating animals like bold little roughhead blennies, vividly colored juvenile queen angelfish and corkscrew anemones with their symbiotic Pederson cleaner shrimp. Of course, you may also come across old Herman, the green moray for which the site is named.

37 FLAGLER'S BARGE

Location: *1.6 nautical miles (3km) northeast of Sombrero Key*
Depth Range: *10-20ft (3-6m)*
Access: *Boat*
Expertise Rating: *Novice*

If you like a dive where you can take your time and poke into every nook and cranny, you'll probably love Flagler's Barge. This shallow site allows plenty of bottom time and the old barge is packed with fish life and marine invertebrates. Mount the macro lens on your camera or video and have fun. Fish watchers will enjoy this site, too, with or without a camera. High-hats, normally difficult to find and photograph, swim freely

Southern stingray buried in the sand for a snooze

in large numbers. Mixed schools of bluestriped, French and Caesar grunts, mangrove snappers, schoolmasters and yellowtail goatfish crowd the interior compartments.

Also called the 'Delta Shoal Barge' or simply 'the Barge', the exact origin of the vessel is unknown. It probably carried construction materials and supplies to Marathon during repair work on Flagler's Overseas Railroad in the 1920s or '30s. One hundred feet long and 30ft wide, it sits in 20ft of water on a flat sand bottom. Both ends slope upward, a design that allowed it to be towed in either direction. Much of the side plating has corroded away, leaving an exposed framework of steel I-beams that support the remaining deck and hull sections. Caribbean giant anemones adorn the hull and crossbeams and the interior is liberally coated with white telesto corals

and a colorful assortment of encrusting sponges. The entire wreck is easily accessible to divers and snorkelers.

If you tire of fish-watching on the barge, take a swim around the surrounding terrain. Nurse sharks and rays often rest on the sand, and the turtle grass beds boast an ecology all their own.

38 | DELTA SHOAL

Location: *1 nautical mile (1.9km) east northeast of Sombrero Reef*
Depth Range: *7-25ft (2-8m)*
Access: *Boat*
Expertise Rating: *Novice*

The remains of a navigation tower lie scattered over the shallowest portion of Delta Shoal, in about 7ft of water. In the same area, a slave ship now known as the Ivory Coast Wreck ran aground in 1853. Only a determined search will locate any sign of the old ship now, but numerous artifacts were recovered here in the past. Some maintain that the name of the wreck comes from ivory tusks salvaged after the grounding, perhaps confusing this wreck with the *Henrietta Marie,* a 1699 slave ship discovered by Mel Fisher well to the west of Delta Shoal.

Like most Florida reefs, Delta Shoal consists of a series of coral-covered ridges, aligned perpendicular to the distant shore. Schooling tomtates and French grunts are particularly numerous along the sides and on top of the fingers. Rock beauties and queen angelfish are also abundant, placidly munching on clustered brown tube and orange elephant ear sponges. The maximum depth at the seaward end of the ridges is just below 25ft.

Orange elephant ear sponge

It's possible to tour the entire reef on one dive, but you'd miss much of the scenery. A better way to see a shallow reef like this is to stay in one place. Anchor yourself next to a coral ridge with one fin tip resting gently in the sand, cross your arms and relax. Stay as motionless as possible, breathing lightly and evenly. You may feel foolish, but within a few minutes the fish will grow accustomed to your presence, stop perceiving you as a possible threat, and the reef will come alive.

39 SOMBRERO REEF

Location: *3.5 nautical miles (6.7km) south of Boot Key*
Depth Range: *6-75ft (2-23m)*
Access: *Boat*
Expertise Rating: *Intermediate*

Named by early Spanish explorers, Sombrero Reef is almost directly offshore from the east end of the Seven Mile Bridge. The reef is marked by the 142ft Sombrero Key Light, which can easily be seen from the highway. Built in 1858, before the key itself eroded away, the light was automated in 1960 and still operates as an aid to navigation.

The main feature of Sombrero Reef is an extensive spur-and-groove system. Long, parallel coral-topped ridges are aligned laterally across the reef, separated by low sand channels. The depth at the shallow end is about 6ft to the top of the spurs and 10ft to the sand. Maximum depth along the ends of the spurs is about 30ft. Although a compass is useful, divers can navigate easily at Sombrero by keeping count as they cross the coral spurs. Out six, return six and you should be back at your boat.

Most of the living coral cover is atop the spurs, where exposure to currents and sunlight is greatest, though competition for space relegates some colonies to the sides, as well as on the exposed hard bottom in the sand channels. A wide variety of encrusting sponges, which are not dependent on sunlight, coat the sides and undercut surfaces of the ridges. These colorful sponges are prominently displayed at a feature known as 'the arch,' where an undercut ridge forms a graceful span.

Use caution when surfacing, as Sombrero Reef is one of the few Sanctuary Preservation Areas that allow trolling for fish by boat.

Sombrero Reef Light towers 142ft above the reef

Key West & the Lower Keys

NEWFOUND HARBOR

Location: *0.5 nautical miles (1km) south of Newfound Harbor Keys*
Depth Range: *Surface-18ft (5m)*
Access: *Boat*
Expertise Rating: *Novice*

Closer to shore than most other reefs, this sanctuary preservation area is a good alternative when weather prevents diving at nearby **Looe Key**. Just northwest is low-lying Little Palm Island, now home to an exclusive resort. The namesake palm trees were planted in the '60s to lend the island a South Pacific look when it was used as the setting for the movie *PT-109*.

A series of mooring buoys are in place along the west side of the reef, and day marker 50 lies to the south. The top of the reef is very shallow, rising almost to the surface in two places. Maximum depth is about 8ft (2.4m) on the landward side and 18ft (5m) on the seaward side. Soft corals dominate much of the reef, but boulder-like accumulations of calcium carbonate from hard corals form the basic structure.

Fishermen frequented the reef until the summer of 1997 when the SPA went into effect, and the resident fish population has been steadily increasing ever

Key West & Lower Keys

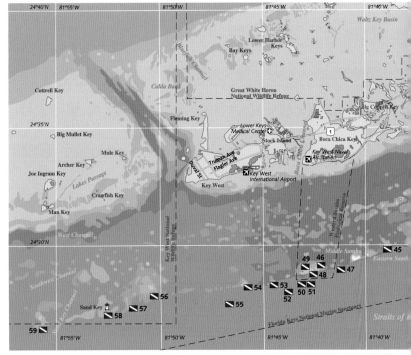

Key West & the Lower Keys	GOOD SNORKELING	NOVICE	INTERMEDIATE	ADVANCED
40 NEWFOUND HARBOR	•	•		
41 LOOE KEY (EAST)	•		•	
42 LOOE KEY (DEEP)			•	
43 LOOE KEY (WEST)	•		•	
44 ADOLPHUS BUSCH SR				•
45 SAM'S REEF	•	•		
46 CANNONBALL CUT	•	•		
47 SECRET REEF			•	
48 HAYSTACKS	•	•		
49 FINGERS	•	•		
50 ARCH			•	
51 CABLE			•	
52 JOE'S TUG			•	
53 TOPPINO'S BUOY	•	•		
54 NINE FOOT STAKE	•	•		

Key West & the Lower Keys	GOOD SNORKELING	NOVICE	INTERMEDIATE	ADVANCED
55 CAYMAN SALVAGE MASTER				•
56 EASTERN DRY ROCKS	•	•		
57 ROCK KEY	•	•		
58 SAND KEY REEF	•		•	
59 WESTERN DRY ROCKS	•	•		
60 MARQUESAS KEYS	•		•	

Caesar and French grunts

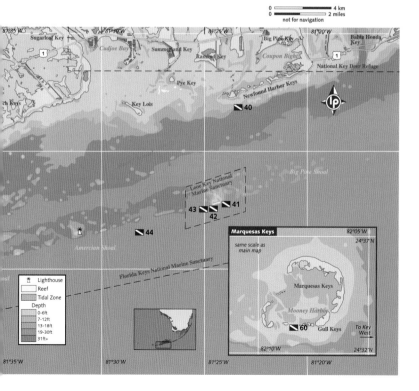

since. Snappers and grunts in particular have benefited from the additional protection. Gray snappers and Caesar grunts are found here in large numbers, along with occasional mutton snappers and French grunts. Like most inshore reefs, Newfound Harbor is also a nursery ground for the outer reefs, and juveniles of many reef fish are present.

Currents near shore give the water a greenish cast and limit visibility to about 20ft, though visibility improves during incoming tides and periods of low wind. When the winds are up, reduced visibility is a reasonable trade-off for this site's calm dive conditions.

Red-spotted hawfish

41 LOOE KEY (EAST)

Location: *4.5 nautical miles (8.6km) south of Newfound Harbor Keys*
Depth Range: *10-35ft (3-11m)*
Access: *Boat*
Expertise Rating: *Intermediate*

Looe Key takes its name from the wreck of HMS *Looe,* a 46-gun frigate built in 1741.

Commanded by Capt Ashby Utting, the warship was sent to protect British interests along the Florida and Georgia coastlines. In 1744 the *Looe* crew captured a suspected Spanish vessel sailing under a French flag and took the ship under tow. But early on the morning of February 5, the *Looe* ran aground on the east end of the reef. Remnants of the ship remain at about 25ft, though don't expect to find them without a knowledgeable guide.

The reef consists of parallel limestone ridges, built up over the past five or six thousand years from the excreted calcium carbonate of coral polyps. Living coral flourishes atop these ridges and on isolated coral heads in the sand channels between them. The depth is about 10ft near the reef crest, sloping to 35ft at the end of the ridges.

Although hard corals such as star and brain corals thrive here, there is also a healthy concentration of soft corals. Common sea fans grow at all depths, while sea plumes, sea rods and sea whips are plentiful below 15ft. Many soft corals look so much like trees, it's easy to forget they are colonial animals like hard corals. Soft corals, though, have flexible skeletons and their polyps feature eight tentacles, instead of six as on the hard corals.

Naturally, this is also a good spot to find invertebrates that feed on gorgonians, like distinctively patterned flamingo tongues or the spiky bristle worms. Look for these creatures near the base of the colony or along one of the arms. Avoid

Key Deer

As you drive south on the Overseas Hwy, you're first exposure to Key Deer is likely to be the rigidly enforced lower speed limit on Big Pine Key. Most of the 800 or so Key Deer live in the National Key Deer Refuge on Big Pine, where a visitors center allows close-up viewing. Thought to have been stranded in the Keys six to 12 thousand years ago by glacial melting, these unique creatures are like miniature deer, standing only a bit over two feet tall at the shoulder.

Parrotfish at a cleaning station

the temptation to handle any of these intriguing invertebrates – in addition to being protected, many of them will surprise you with a painful sting.

42 LOOE KEY (DEEP)

Location: *4.5 nautical miles (8.6km) south of Newfound Harbor Keys*
Depth Range: *40-80ft (12-24m)*
Access: *Boat*
Expertise Rating: *Intermediate*

Seaward of the dramatic coral ridges of the Looe Key fore reef, the underwater terrain gives way to a gently sloping plain, ending in the sand at about 80ft. At first glance it may look dull, but what you're seeing is a fertile transition zone – from big corals to big sponges and high-profile ridges to low fingers and narrow sand channels.

This is the deep reef, where you're more likely to encounter a free-swimming Spanish mackerel or cobia than the schools of grunts or snappers that are common on the fore reef. Parrotfish poke around in small groups and angelfish cruise by in pairs, but the big aggregations are not to be found here. The same holds true for the corals. Hard corals are still present – they're just low-profile and spread out at this depth. Sea plumes and sea rods, on the other hand, grow taller here than in the shallows. Beginning around 50ft you'll find colonies of deepwater sea fans.

Sponges are plentiful, including many giant barrel sponges. It's difficult to swim past their tall chimneys without taking a peek inside. Most are empty, as the interior is the excurrent opening – the output vent of the sponge's digestive system. Occasionally you'll find something surprising, like a green moray, a channel clinging crab or even a colony of Porites coral. Periodically, on some as yet unknown timetable, the sponges reproduce en masse, expelling smoky clouds of eggs or sperm.

Navigation is easy on the deep reef, as the parallel ridges and sand channels are still present, though less prominent than on the fore reef. Following the channels will take you to either deeper or shallower water, and crossing the ridges will take you laterally across the reef. Strong currents are common at this site.

43	LOOE KEY (WEST)

Location: *4.5 nautical miles (8.6km) south of Newfound Harbor Keys*
Depth Range: *Surface-35ft (11m)*
Access: *Boat*
Expertise Rating: *Intermediate*

The west end of this classic outer-bank reef supports a greater build-up of boulder corals than the east end. A high-profile spur-and-groove formation begins in 10ft to 12ft of water, sloping to 35ft at the seaward end. Huge colonies of brain, star and giant star corals grow one on top of the other – national treasures on a par with California's great redwoods. Many of these masters of reef building have been alive for more than three centuries.

Toward the reef crest the ridges are narrow and close together, the channel between them only 2ft or 3ft wide in some places. Deep undercuts are common, usually lined with rows of clustered brown tube or orange elephant ear sponges. As some of the star and brain coral heads on this reef approach the limits of their age, they have been invaded by other animals, such as orange icing sponge and red boring sponge. Both of these organisms bore into the coral, lifting the edges and cutting away at the coral's structure.

The shallow, rubble-capped reef crest gives way to an expansive back reef of sand flats and thick seagrass beds. Even snorkelers must exercise caution near the reef crest, where depths can be less than a foot. The abundance of white encrusting zoanthids, *Palythoa caribaeorum*, in this zone may be another sign of the reef's old age.

Fishing and lobstering have been prohibited here for three decades, and the fish have grown accustomed to divers. As you swim through aggregations of yellowtail snappers, sergeant majors,

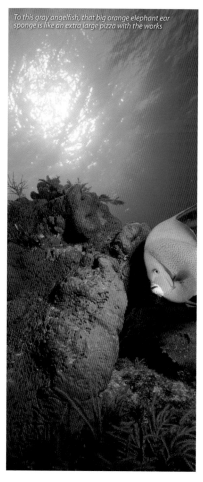
To this gray angelfish, that big orange elephant ear sponge is like an extra large pizza with the works

surgeonfish and French grunts, they will barely expend the energy to get out of your way. Larger fish, like barracuda, mutton snappers and Nassau groupers, will eyeball you cautiously but hold their ground.

---

44 ADOLPHUS BUSCH SR

Location: *3.5 nautical miles (6.7km) west of Looe Key*
Depth Range: *70-115 ft (21-35m)*
Access: *Boat*
Expertise Rating: *Advanced*

The *Busch* has held together well over the years since she was sunk on December 5, 1998. Built in Scotland in 1951, this 210ft coastal freighter sailed the Atlantic, Great Lakes and Caribbean under the names *London*, *Windsor Trader*, *Topsail Star* and *Ocean Alley* before the Looe Key Artificial Reef Association found her languishing at the dock in Port-au-Prince, Haiti. With the generous support of Adolphus Busch IV, the association purchased the vessel and towed it to Miami for an extensive clean-up and preparations to make it diver safe. Oil, fuel and other possible contaminants

The wreck of the Busch

were removed, along with hatches and doors that might impede diver egress. The ship, renamed *Adolphus Busch Sr* after the patriarch of the brewing family, was carefully anchored a few miles west of Looe Key and gently scuttled in 115ft of water. She landed upright on the sandy bottom, secured in position by two bow anchors and one stern anchor. Because of the depth and frequent strong currents, local dive shops may require proof of advanced certification and recently logged deep dives.

Four mooring buoys are arrayed along the starboard side of the ship. In order to prevent visitor conflicts, two buoys are reserved for diving and two for fishing. The shallowest spot on the wreck is a small mast on the wheelhouse, about 70ft deep. It's about 75ft to the top of the stack and 80ft to the top of the wheelhouse. The main deck is at 90ft and the sandy bottom near the single propeller is just shy of 115ft.

With all the doors and hatches removed, you can swim right down into the open holds and explore the tiered decks around their perimeter. A dive light will come in handy even though the ship is fairly open. A well-encrusted mast and anchor windlass add some interest to the bow.

The *Busch* demonstrates how effective a shipwreck can be as an artificial reef. Reef fish swarm all over the wreck, especially around the wheelhouse, where thousands of Caesar grunts have taken up residence. A gang of great barracuda roam the wreck, and a pair of large jewfish have called the *Busch* home for several years. Sharks are frequently sighted here as well, including the occasional hammerhead.

After diving the wreck, go out and rent a copy of *Fire Down Below*, the 1957 film starring Robert Mitchum, Jack Lemmon and Rita Hayworth, to see the *Busch* in her previous life. The disaster staged on the ship for the movie seems a haunting premonition of things to come.

45 SAM'S REEF

Location: *4.5 nautical miles (8.6km) south of Boca Chica Key*
Depth Range: *Surface to 25ft (8m)*
Access: *Boat*
Expertise Rating: *Novice*

Sam's Reef is a favorite for dive instructors because it has a large sandy arena where students can gather to practice and demonstrate their diving skills. Even if you're not part of a class, Sam's Reef can be a delightful dive or snorkel. When the wind is blowing though, expect lowered visibility due to particles suspended in the water.

The temptation might be to try and cover a lot of territory on dives here, since the coral cover is somewhat less than other sites in the area, but a better strategy is simply to slow down. Focus on a narrower part of the reef and you'll discover that it's as full of life as anywhere else.

A sharp eye will see the critters that hide from casual observers, including reef octopus, scorpionfish, lettuce leaf slugs and redlip blennies. Sometimes the most barren looking part of a reef, especially a shallow reef, is actually the most prolific. Take the time to examine every part of the reef, including the rubble zones and sand patches. Gobies, nudibranches, bristleworms and other interesting sea creatures are often in the most unlikely looking places.

Coral Spawning

Elkhorn coral spawning

Corals reproduce in several interesting ways. One is simply by breaking off, an accidental approach that allows branching corals in particular to occupy more space. Individual polyps also split into two, a cloning mechanism that accounts for the way coral boulders and branches grow. The most fascinating method of coral reproduction however, is called mass (or broadcast) spawning.

Broadcast spawning of corals in the Florida Keys occurs primarily in August, triggered by the full moon. Branching corals, such as elkhorn and antler coral, spawn three to five days after the August full moon, simultaneously releasing eggs and sperm into the water. The event is always at night, usually two to four hours after dusk.

The biggest show is put on by the boulder corals, such as star coral, *Montastrea annularis*. Star corals wait until six to eight days after the August full moon, then release gametes in a frenzy that can turn the water milky. The boulder coral mass spawning also occurs two to four hours after dusk.

46 CANNONBALL CUT

Location: *4.5 nautical miles (8.6km) south of Boca Chica Key*
Depth Range: *10-30ft (3-10m)*
Access: *Boat*
Expertise Rating: *Novice*

Named after a natural cut in the reef and for the scattered cannonballs and ballast stones found in the area, this dive site is part of the Western Sambo Ecological Reserve (ER). An ER is similar to a Sanctuary Preservation Area (SPA), but larger and intended to provide sheltered spawning and nursery areas for a variety of marine life. If the acronyms glaze your eyes over, just think of it as a breeding ground for all the critters you hope to see when you strap that tank on.

The largest coral ridges are immediately north of the mooring, in the direction of land. The ballast stones, as you might expect, can be found in these shallow areas. They were deposited there following a ship grounding, either immediately after the incident or after the wooden timbers rotted away.

South of the mooring is somewhat deeper water with smaller, more scat-

Shallow corals always attract a lot of fish

tered coral heads among areas of sand and coral rubble. Star, starlet and brain corals are represented here, as well as some very nice pillar coral along the 30ft contour. Schools of blue tang and surgeonfish comb the area looking for some nice algae to eat, as well as loose bands of parrotfish.

47 SECRET REEF

Location: *4.5 nautical miles (8.6km) south of Boca Chica Key*
Depth Range: *30-65ft (10-20m)*
Access: *Boat*
Expertise Rating: *Intermediate*

Tall coral ridges meander across a gradual slope on this expansive reef. It's easy to get turned around while following one of the ridges, particularly if you come across a turtle, nurse shark or some other animal that leads you further and further from the boat. However, that same physical complexity makes this reef a superb habitat.

The undercuts, swim-through, ledges and mini-canyons cut into these ridges may contain nearly every species found in the Keys. Bright blue parrotfish roam in packs, pale mangrove snapper huddle under the overhangs, queen angelfish munch on the elephant ear sponges and banded butterflyfish peck at the coral. Hard corals include lovely cones of star coral, healthy specimens of convoluted brain coral and smooth golden globes of starlet coral.

As with other dives in the Keys, the slower you go, the more you'll see. Let the fish get used to your bubble-blowing presence and they'll actually come right up to your mask and look you in the eye. Slowing down, or even stopping for 10 or 15 minutes, seems difficult for many of us, but it's worth the time.

48 HAYSTACKS

Location: *4.5 nautical miles (8.6km) south of Boca Chica Key*
Depth Range: *20-35ft (6-11m)*
Access: *Boat*
Expertise Rating: *Novice*

The name Haystacks describes the general shape and size of the star corals found here, but it doesn't acknowledge the majesty of these colonial animals. Few of us probably think in terms of majesty when we see a huge greenish brown mound underwater, but what else would you call a creature that has been alive for three centuries? When these coral heads were youngsters, Florida belonged to Spain and the colony of Virginia was celebrating the birth of a child named George Washington.

Starting with a single larval polyp, these colonies have grown in diameter by a scant half an inch (1cm) per year, somehow surviving over the centuries to reach their present regal size. If you see some with a few scars here and there, consider that the price of a long life, like giant redwoods with a couple of broken limbs.

Of course even these lovely star corals are not the whole story to this reef. As you tour the Haystacks, you'll see globes of smooth brain coral, convoluted brain coral and starlet coral. A

Sponge Spawning

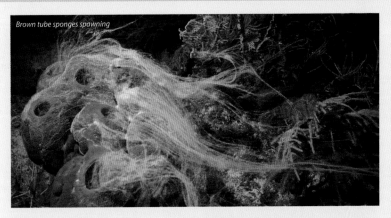

Brown tube sponges spawning

Like corals, many species of sponge utilize mass spawning for reproduction. In the Keys, the giant barrel sponge and brown tube sponge are the most commonly observed. Little is known about the mechanism that triggers a spawning event in sponges, however it is probably tied to phases of the moon.

Some sponges are hermaphrodites and simply shed eggs already fertilized by sperm into the water. Others, like the barrel sponge, are either male or female. During a mass spawning event, the males pump clouds of sperm like smokestacks. The females produce heavier eggs, which tend to collect inside the sponge where they are fertilized by the cloud of released sperm.

Sponge spawning has not been well documented, but events have been observed in March, July, August and December.

lone patch of pillar coral can be found at a depth of about 25ft, on the western side of the reef.

In the end, every coral reef is about the food chain. The coral polyps, sponges and algae bring fish, which in turn bring fish to eat the fish. You can see them all here at one time or another, but the sure sightings are butterflyfish, parrotfish, grunts and jacks. Sightings of southern stingrays, spotted morays and hawksbill turtles are also a strong possibility.

49   FINGERS

Location: *4.5 nautical miles (8.6km) south of Boca Chica Key*
Depth Range: *5-20ft (2-6m)*
Access: *Boat*
Expertise Rating: *Novice*

Divers can poke around the Fingers at the end of a dive, but the site is primarily for snorkelers. The main feature of the area is provided by the parallel ridges, or fingers, of coral. Two hands worth of fingers, actually.

Unless the weather is absolutely calm, expect a bit of surge here because of the shallow depth. That surge is exactly why the soft corals, branching hard corals and sponges are growing here. A constant supply of food is carried across the reef with each whoosh of water. The corals in turn attract fish – a lot of fish. This is a great reef to carry one of those plastic fish ID cards and see how many of them you can spot.

The bottom between the fingers is either sand, coral rubble or exposed fossil reef bed. Although it may look somewhat barren at first glance, a closer view will reveal numerous small gobies and blennies and many species of marine invertebrates. You'll have to dive down or be using scuba to appreciate the critters in the grooves, but it's worth a look.

Giant star coral polyps

Hawksbill turtles are often curious about divers

50 | ARCH

Location: *5.5 nautical miles (10km) south of Stock Island*
Depth Range: *35-55ft (7-17m)*
Access: *Boat*
Expertise Rating: *Intermediate*

Sometimes called 'Eye of the Needle' after the narrow swim-through that is the most prominent landmark on the reef, this dive encompasses a sprawling section of low profile coral spurs alternating with fairly narrow sandy channels.

The natural thing to do is swim along the sand channels observing the fish and coral on the coral spurs to your left and right. This is a fine way to see the reef since it puts your eyes at the right level and the sand gives you a place to safely stop if you must. Don't neglect the sand itself, though. Lots of critters make their homes there, especially along the edge near where the coral ridge meets the sand. Little yellowhead jawfish can be seen hovering vertically over their burrows. If you watch patiently, you may even see one of the males incubating a mouthful of silver eggs.

You'll certainly swim over dozens of nearly-translucent bridled gobies, named for the white slash that extends backward from the corner of the jaw. These bold little fish will stand their ground until you're almost eyeball to eyeball, then they'll shoot a couple of feet away and make another stand.

Determined divers can reach deeper water by heading south, but the coral cover diminishes beyond 65ft and a

A yellowhead jawfish cleans sand from its hole

broad flat of sand and seagrass begins in about 80ft. This area is filled with interesting invertebrates, but bottom time will be limited. If you reach this area, look out into the void, because larger animals like shark and turtles may cruise past.

51 CABLE

Location: *5.5 nautical miles (10km) south of Stock Island*
Depth Range: *35-65ft (10-20m)*
Access: *Boat*
Expertise Rating: *Intermediate*

This reef dive takes its name from the Key West to Cuba telephone cable still visible across several of the coral fingers.

The cable is part of a system of three cables laid by Western Union in 1921, each about 100 nautical miles long and lying about 1000ft deep at the midpoint. The cable is remarkably well preserved, but you probably won't hear voices if you press your ear to it, as local lore maintains.

The coral fingers run generally north and south, so they make a good guide as you navigate the reef. Deeper water is to the south, shallower to the north. The fingers get less prominent as you head toward deep water, but they can still be followed.

The hard corals have a lower profile than similar species on shallower reefs, but most colonies are in good condition. One of the best features of this reef is the sponge life. The largest specimens are the giant barrel and leathery barrel sponges, but if you pay attention you'll see many others. Take a close look at any branching gray vase sponges you find and see if they are carrying any additional riders. Quite often these sponges have been inflicted with parasitic zoanthids, a tiny creature that looks like a little brown sea anemone.

The presence of sponges inevitably means you'll encounter several other animals, including the oddly shaped

A mixed school of blue-striped grunts and yellow goatfish

arrow crab. Watch for these critters at the base of sponges or even inside the sponge. Hawksbill turtles and angelfish are also drawn to areas with abundant sponge life, since sponges form a significant part of their diets. Gray and French angelfish seem to reside in particularly large numbers here.

If you keep heading south, the reef will eventually slope into deeper water, but the coral cover dissipates rather quickly beyond 65ft.

52 JOE'S TUG

Location: *5.5 nautical miles (10km) south of Stock Island*
Depth Range: *50-65ft (15-20m)*
Access: *Boat*
Expertise Rating: *Intermediate*

Hurricane Wilma in 2005 was not kind to Joe's Tug, but to be fair other hurricanes had already been steadily disman-

tling the little ship. In 1998, Hurricane Georges tore off the wheelhouse, depositing most of it upside down on the port side. A year later Hurricane Irene cracked the hull amidships. The ocean also did her share, corroding the rudderpost until the big rudder eventually fell to the bottom. Today the wreck is more of a debris field than a ship, but it still attracts a lot of fish, and the surrounding reef alone is worth the dive.

The wreck began life as a steel harbor tug about 75ft long, built with a small wheelhouse well forward and a clear afterdeck. After a steady but undistinguished career, the tug was retired in old age and ignominiously sunk at her dock in the Safe Harbor Marina in 1986. Stripped of its engine and propeller and filled with scraps of steel, it was destined for duty as an artificial reef off Miami. The details of how she came to sink prematurely in 60ft of water south of Key West on January 21, 1989, have blurred over the years, like other interesting bits of Key West history. Imagine more than a few ounces of rum and a dark-of-the-night liberation tow and you get the general idea. 'Rediscovered' after the dust settled, Joe's Tug became one of Key West's favorite dives due to its moderate depth, excellent fish life and good surrounding reef. The resident schools of grunts and snapper, a resident jewfish and frequent turtle sightings remain highlights of the area. The reef always beckons too, with nice colonies of star and brain coral as well as many giant barrel sponges and leather barrel sponges.

53 TOPPINO'S BUOY

Location: *5 nautical miles (9.5km) south of Stock Island*
Depth Range: *12-30ft (4-9m)*
Access: *Boat*
Expertise Rating: *Novice*

This site is also known as 'Marker One', even though the navigation aid at the site is clearly marked with the number 32. The Marker One name goes back to the time of the ferries, when the navigational aid at this reef was the first marker seen by ferryboat captains bound for Key West. The main structure of the reef is a parallel series of eight coral fingers, oriented north and south, with a ninth ridge oriented east-west in the middle. In the shallow part of the reef, depths are about 12ft to the top of the coral and 22ft in the sand. From the seaward end of the fingers a hard bottom slopes into deeper water, though it's a long swim by the time you reach 30ft. The flats are sprinkled with moderate-sized hard and soft corals, but most of the sea life can be found between the fingers.

Hundreds of fish hang about the coral walls, not separated by species, but mixed into one constantly milling mass. Margates, scrawled filefish, banded butterflyfish, bluestriped grunts, sur-

geonfish, smallmouth grunts and gray snappers all mingle together, weaving a colorful tapestry. You might see a pair of spotfin butterflyfish pecking at one coral head and a pair of foureye butterflyfish right next door. The ledges also attract larger animals, like nurse sharks and hawksbill turtles, especially early in the morning or in the evening.

Toppino's is a popular night dive, as it's shallow and marked by a navigation light. All three buoys are positioned at the deep end of the coral fingers, evenly spaced across the reef. Divers can easily find their way along the reef by keeping track of the fingers.

At night a whole new cast of characters takes the stage. Eels that hid shyly during the day may be out hunting under cover of darkness. Channel crabs, lobster, brittle stars and tarpon are active, too. Your dive light brings out the reds, purples and oranges that the phenomenon of selective absorption robbed from the sun, so everything looks different. Even if you make a day dive the same afternoon, you'll hardly recognize the place at night.

Nurse sharks are often observed by divers in the Keys

54 NINE FOOT STAKE

Location: *5 nautical miles (9.5km) south of Key West*
Depth Range: *9-25ft (3-7m)*
Access: *Boat*
Expertise Rating: *Novice*

Coral ledges are what make this dive interesting. The site is composed of a double row of coral fingers, six in very shallow water with another grouping in slightly deeper water to the south. All these coral fingers have been undercut by age and tide, creating countless homes and hiding places for fish and invertebrates. Add the encrusting and boring sponges that brighten up the underside of the ledges with hues of orange and red, and the result is an extremely enjoyable experience for both divers and snorkelers.

One of the largest coral colonies here is a massive head of smooth brain coral, so old that most of its foundation has eroded. When you see it, try to calculate its age, considering that a boulder coral formation grows about 1cm in diameter each year. When you come up with a number, you'll probably have the urge to reverently say, 'Good

afternoon, Grandfather,' and swim away respectfully.

Spiny lobsters, spotted morays, stoplight parrotfish and foureye butterflyfish are common here, but many divers flock here to see its smaller residents. Macro photographers in particular love this reef. Take any 10 sq ft section and you'll find lots of juvenile reef fish and marine invertebrates for subjects. At night the selection gets even better. Without trying very hard you can find red night shrimp, stareye hermit crabs, arrow crabs, lettuce sea slugs, scorpionfish and red-spotted hawkfish, just to name a few.

55 CAYMAN SALVAGE MASTER

Location: *5.5 nautical miles (10km) south of Key West*
Depth Range: *65-90ft (20-27m)*
Access: *Boat*
Expertise Rating: *Advanced*

The *Cayman Salvage Master* was built in 1937 by Pusey & Jones shipyard in Wilmington, Delaware, as a minelayer for the US Army Mine Planter Service, and was originally named the *Lt Col Ellery W Niles*. In 1945 she was transferred to the Army

A spotted moray shows its needle-like teeth

Divers return to the mooring line for the ascent after exploring the Cayman Salvage Master

Signal Corps for service as a cable layer. In 1965 she was purchased by Marine Acoustical Services of Miami and re-named FV *Hunt*. Before ending up on the bottom off Key West, she was also a research vessel for TRACOR of Miami, a freighter under Panamanian registry and, in her final incarnation, a salvage vessel under Cayman Islands registry.

In 1980 the ship was confiscated by the US Government for illegally carrying Cuban refugees during the Mariel Boatlift. The next three years were spent tied to the dock in Key West, until the ship sank in place from neglect. After she was refloated, her pilothouse was removed, and the vessel was slated to be sunk in deep water, primarily as a fish magnet for sport fishing. On the way to the designated site in April 1985, the *Cayman Salvage Master* again sank prematurely, landing on her port side in 90ft of water. Later that same year, in a precursor to the amazing righting of the mighty *Spiegel Grove* off Key Largo, storm surge from Hurricane Kate rolled the ship upright.

The *Cayman Salvage Master* is 187ft in length with a 37ft beam. Minus its superstructure, the wreck still rises 26ft from the bottom. As the starboard hull rested face up for the first half year after the ship sank, that side in particular is covered with swaying soft corals. The spoked cable spool still graces the bow and is a focal point on the wreck, always surrounded by schools of grunts, jacks and damselfish.

Although some openings breach the hull, the *Cayman Salvage Master* is not a good wreck for penetration. Thick cables and other obstacles block

56 EASTERN DRY ROCKS

Location: *2 nautical miles (3.8km) east northeast of Sand Key*
Depth Range: *Surface-30ft (9m)*
Access: *Boat*
Expertise Rating: *Novice*

This is a favorite spot for snorkel boats out of Key West. The combination of high visitation and strong surge has reduced the live coral cover over the years, but much of the reef is still healthy, and there are lots of fish. Eastern Dry Rock has been a Sanctuary Preservation Area for nearly a decade, allowing the fish population time to grow.

The reef crest at Eastern Dry Rocks is three quarters of a mile long, oriented generally east-west. Most of the mooring buoys are along the west end of the reef, which is generally the leeward side. One additional buoy is on the back reef.

New elkhorn coral recruits have sprouted up in several places, particularly in the shallows along the southern edge. These new colonies grow upward at a 45-degree angle in branches less than a foot long. Take care not to kick them, as they'll break easily, destroying two or three years worth of growth.

the entrances, and there is very little maneuvering room inside. Strong currents are common.

As you head east from the mooring buoys, you'll cross several dozen parallel fingers of coral that make up the structure of the reef. To the north, the reef gives way to flats of finely ground coral rubble, sand and seagrass. A variety of invertebrates and juvenile fish live in this zone, and a wide range of herbivores depend on it for food. To the south, the reef slopes quickly down to 30ft, then eases down to 70ft or 75ft. Most of the coral is concentrated in the top 30ft, though more soft corals and sponges reside in the lower half.

A scrawled filefish shelters beneath an elkhorn coral branch

Trumpetfish, *Aulostomus maculates*, one of the reef's most voracious predators

57 **ROCK KEY**

Location: *1 nautical mile (1.9km) east of Sand Key*
Depth Range: *Surface-30ft (9m)*
Access: *Boat*
Expertise Rating: *Novice*

A diamond-shaped day marker warns of shallow water on this reef, which is located about midway between **Sand Key** and **Eastern Dry Rocks**. The marker is well warranted, as the reef crest is exposed at low tide. The best diving is between 10ft and 30ft, along a prominent sand channel that runs through the middle of the reef. Ridges on the west side form a canyon with deeply undercut sides. The undersides of the ledges are painted bright yellow and orange by encrusting sponges, though the colors only come alive when lit by a strobe or powerful dive light. Below 30ft the live coral cover is sparse, and the bottom is flat.

Rock Key is one of 18 sanctuary preservation areas in the Keys. The prohibition against all means of marine life harvesting, including hook-and-line fishing, has dramatically increased the fish population. Yellowtail snappers, bluestriped grunts and sergeant majors are among the most abundant, but all of the common species are present.

This site presents a good alternative when all the buoys are taken at **Sand Key**, but the low percentage of live coral cover may disappoint some. It's a nice spot when you don't want to exert a lot of energy swimming. You can take it easy here and still see most of the reef.

The reef is extensive, with the parallel coral fingers and alternating sand channels typical of outer Florida Keys reefs. Only a few feet deep at the shallowest sections, Sand Key is great for snorkelers who just want to float on the surface and enjoy the show below. The deep end of the coral fingers is in about 35ft of water.

Move slowly to approach the myriad of reef fish that feed on suspended plankton. Sergeant majors often feed in large schools near the surface, along with dozens of yellowtail snappers, Creole wrasses and brown chromis. Closer to the reef, several species of damselfish defend their territory, and slender trumpetfish skulk among the coral branches in hope of ambushing smaller fish.

Visibility is highly variable at Sand Key due to strong surge and tidal flow. If you happen to visit when the water is cloudy, don't count it out – next time the conditions may be splendid.

The lighthouse at Sand Key is another historic reef light. Constructed in 1853, the light has survived many storms that temporarily removed all the sand from Sand Key. It was automated in 1941 and a fire destroyed the lighthouse keeper's dwelling in 1989, but the light is still in operation.

58   SAND KEY REEF

Location: *6.5 nautical miles (12km) southwest of Key West*
Depth Range: *5-35ft (2-11m)*
Access: *Boat*
Expertise Rating: *Intermediate*

Sand Key is one of Key West's most popular snorkel spots. The shallow reef, sand island and towering lighthouse make it a wonderful place to spend a morning or afternoon taking in the sights above and below water. The exposed sand island is actually pulverized coral and shells. It does not support any vegetation and has shifted considerably in size, shape and location duriing the years.

Trumpetfish are adept at hiding among the corals

Squirrelfish let you approach, but stay close to their holes

59 | WESTERN DRY ROCKS

Location: *3 nautical miles (5.7km) west of Sand Key*
Depth Range: *Surface-40ft (12m)*
Access: *Boat*
Expertise Rating: *Novice*

Suitable for both diving and snorkeling, this reef is still a favorite. The shallowest corals extend much further north than on other reefs, with many interesting nooks for snorkelers to explore. The coral ridges are so shallow that you can simply float at the surface to enjoy the marine life below. Recent storms have taken a toll on the shallow growing elkhorn and staghorn corals on the top of the ridges, and you may notice dead elkhorn branches, gray in color with a light film of algae. It's all part of a natural cycle, and if you look closely you'll see new elkhorn colonies growing in replacement. In the meantime, even the dead colonies provide habitat and food for many fish. The tiny bicolor damselfish, for instance, zealously guards a 'crop' of algae growth on the branches. Get too close and these fearless little fish will dart out and remind you not to trespass with a quick nip on the arm.

More accomplished snorkelers and divers can follow the many fractured ledges that wind through the reef like mini-canyons in 10ft to 15ft of water. These cuts are the main feature of the reef, attracting large numbers of schoolmaster, French grunts, bluestriped grunts and squirrelfish. The whole area has a welcoming brightness, partly from the sunlight that easily penetrates the shallow water and partly from the many red and yellow encrusting sponges.

Head south from the reef crest to reach deeper water. The gradual slope features a fairly smooth, hard bottom sprinkled with medium-sized mounds of starlet and brain corals and a variety of gorgonians. Below 30ft you'll find more sponges, especially smaller giant barrel sponges. Going deeper than 35ft or 40ft requires a lengthy swim away from the moorings atop the reef.

60 MARQUESAS KEYS

Location: 16 nautical miles (30km) west of Key West
Depth Range: Surface-20ft (6m)
Access: Boat
Expertise Rating: Intermediate

This isolated mini-archipelago was used by the military for many years as a bombing and strafing range, but the entire group of islands is now protected within the Key West National Wildlife Refuge.

Other than one or two privately owned houses, the islands are unde-veloped. The surrounding waters, while very shallow, are excellent areas for diving and snorkeling with many interesting wrecks and scattered reefs. Several boats come out to the Marquesas from Key West, but since it's a long run, the trip is typically offered as a whole-day adventure with lunch on the beach.

Currents can be strong during peak tidal flow, especially in the narrow cuts. Those same currents carry an abundance of food to sessile filter feeders, however, making the atoll a great place to find invertebrates like feather duster worms, Christmas tree worms and sea anemones. As the islands sit between the Gulf of Mexico and Straits of Florida, you'll likely encounter species from both areas.

On the trip out to the Marquesas from Key West, you'll pass close to the site where the Spanish treasure galleon, *Nuestra Señora de Atocha,* foundered in 1622. The wreck was located by Mel Fisher in 1985 after years of searching. Artifacts from the historic ship, including gold bars, coins, weapons and delicate jewelry, are on display at his museum in Key West.

A magnificent feather duster worm claims an oasis in the middle of a brain coral

A grove of Christmas tree
worms on a colony of star coral

Fort Jefferson National Monument & the Dry Tortugas

Sunset in the Dry Tortugas

In 1513 Ponce de León gave the name Las Tortugas (the Turtles) to these remote islands due to the large number of resident turtles. More pragmatic sailors noted the lack of fresh water and added 'Dry' to the name. Fifty-five nautical miles (105km) beyond Key West, the archipelago's seven islands are now protected by the Dry Tortugas National Park and the Florida Keys National Marine Sanctuary.

In the early 1800s, the islands of the Dry Tortugas were considered vital to US interests in the Gulf of Mexico, and work was begun on a military installation in 1846. Only partially completed at the start of the Civil War, it remained in Union hands. Sixteen million bricks went into the construction of the fort, and you can still see the difference between the original red bricks, which came from Southern states, and the later orange bricks from the North. The fort never realized any strategic importance, but was used as a prison, counting Lincoln assassination conspirator Dr Samuel Mudd among its inmates. The National Park Service maintains a staff at historic Fort Jefferson and pro-

vides campsites on the beach outside the fort, but visitors to the Dry Tortugas must still be self-sufficient. Access to the islands is by ferry, seaplane, live-aboard or private boat. You can tie up to the dock in front of the fort for a few hours, but for longer stays you must move a short distance to the Garden Key anchorage.

Diving and snorkeling opportunities in the Dry Tortugas are markedly different than in the rest of the Keys. Day visitors can snorkel around the fort on Garden Key, but you'll need a boat to reach other sites like **Windjammer** and **Sherwood Forest**. Much of the diving is on deep, pristine reefs, but their remoteness limits access.

Fort Jefferson National Monument & the Dry Tortugas	GOOD SNORKELING	NOVICE	INTERMEDIATE	ADVANCED
61 SHERWOOD FOREST				•
62 TEXAS ROCK			•	
63 FORT JEFFERSON MOAT WALL		•	•	
64 WINDJAMMER		•	•	

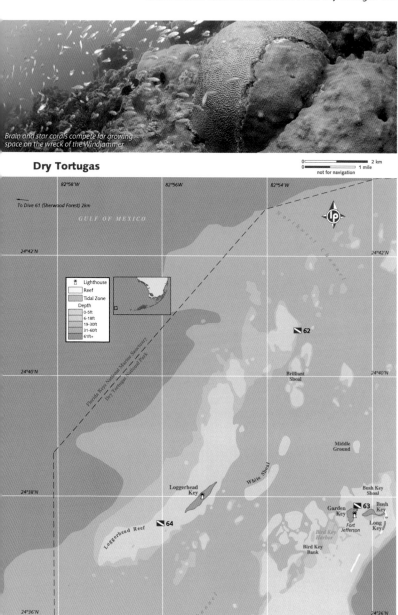

Brain and star corals compete for growing space on the wreck of the Windjammer

Dry Tortugas

0   2 km
0   1 mile
not for navigation

82°58'W   82°56W   82°54'W

To Dive 61 (Sherwood Forest) 2km

GULF OF MEXICO

24°42'N   24°42'N

⚓	Lighthouse
	Reef
	Tidal Zone
	Depth
	0-5ft
	6-18ft
	19-30ft
	31-60ft
	61ft+

◣ 62

Florida Keys National Marine Sanctuary
Dry Tortugas National Park

24°40'N   Brilliant Shoal   24°40'N

Middle Ground

White Shoal

Loggerhead Key   Bush Key Shoal

24°38'N   Garden Key   ◣ 63   Bush Key   24°38'N

◣ 64   Fort Jefferson   Long Key

Loggerhead Reef   *Bird Key Harbor*

Bird Key Bank

24°36'N   24°36'N

SOUTHWEST CHANNEL

82°58'W   82°56W   82°54'W

61 SHERWOOD FOREST

Location: *7 nautical miles (13km) northwest of Loggerhead Key*
Depth Range: *80-100ft (24-30)*
Access: *Boat*
Expertise Rating: *Advanced*

Sherwood Forest is a unique deep reef with a coral canopy, or 'false bottom.' The main reef structure is essentially a shelf about 80ft deep supported by a fossil coral foundation. Below the cracks and hollows you can see the sand bottom another 20ft below.

Colonies of star and giant star corals atop the shelf often grow in tall mushroom shapes to take advantage of the ambient sunlight and prevailing currents. Some of the giant star corals exhibit an unusual fluorescent pigmentation that tints them pinkish red. Several species of black coral also thrive here, often tucked into a small depression or clinging to the side of the shelf. Take extra care not to touch these colonies, as they are very susceptible to damage.

Giant star coral at Sherwood Forest

You'll find the Keys' usual variety of angelfish, snapper, grunts, surgeonfish, damselfish and parrotfish, but you may also see a few surprises in the water column above the coral. Fast-swimming predators like cero and Spanish mackerel often pass by, sometimes swerving for a closer look at divers.

The location and depth of Sherwood Forest usually ensure exceptionally clear, blue water, but the cost of that clarity can be high currents.

62 TEXAS ROCK

Location: *3 nautical miles (5.7km) north northeast of Loggerhead Key*
Depth Range: *Surface-50ft (15m)*
Access: *Boat*
Expertise Rating: *Intermediate*

Only a few miles due north of Garden Key in Dry Tortugas National Park, Texas Rock looks more like Grand Cayman than the Florida Keys. The predictable spur-and-groove formation and gradual slope from shallow to deep is replaced by random peaks and valleys. The sand bottom is about 50ft deep, but much of the reef is less than 18ft deep. The reef face is nearly vertical in most places and often deeply undercut, creating overhangs 10ft and 20ft wide. Unblemished colonies of star and giant star coral grow on top of these meandering ledges, while the underside sprouts a thick beard of deepwater sea fans and tube sponges.

The color orange is prevalent, from numerous grapefruit-sized orange ball sponges to the feathery arms of orange crinoids. The heavy folds of big orange elephant ear sponges also help raise the orange quotient of this reef.

Texas Rock is often swept in moderate currents. Schools of horse-eye jacks and great barracuda circle in the water column adjacent to the reef, while a variety of parrotfish, wrasses and angelfish stick close to the corals. If you have an eye for smaller creatures, you'll also find a wide range of goby and blenny species at Texas Rock.

No wonder it's called an orange elephant ear sponge!

Great snorkeling along
the outside of the moat wall

63 | FORT JEFFERSON MOAT WALL

Location: *Garden Key*
Depth Range: *Surface-20ft (6m)*
Access: *Boat, seaplane, shore*
Expertise Rating: *Novice*

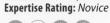

If you're planning to visit Fort Jefferson by ferry or seaplane, be sure to bring your snorkel gear because the outer face of the moat wall surrounding Fort Jefferson is a splendid snorkeling site. Scuba is not recommended, as most depths are only 3ft to 6ft. Entry is from the beach beside the campsites. The

Inside the moat at Fort Jefferson

bottom is mostly sand and seagrass with scattered coral patches, and the water gets progressively deeper as you swim away from the wall. Several hundred yards out are some nice patch reefs in 15ft to 20ft of water, but stay clear of the boat channels leading to the Garden Key anchorage. The best snorkeling is in the shallows, which spar buoys mark off as no-boating zones.

Beside the wall and along the brickwork itself is where you'll find all the action. Expect to come across almost anything, from Caribbean octopuses and pencil urchins, to sea anemones and yellow stingrays. The hard corals are represented mostly by small heads of star and brain coral, but there are plenty of healthy sea fans and sea plumes. Stoplight parrotfish, porkfish and bluestriped grunts dominate the fish population, while star-eyed hermit crabs and queen conch are also plentiful.

Circumnavigating the fort with snorkel and fins is a fascinating adventure. Watch for boat traffic near the dock and a short stretch beside the channel, but the rest of the route is clear. Sand shoals now block the channel adjacent to the old coal dock to all traffic except very small boats. The pilings of the old dock are coated with sponges and corals and packed with fish, including huge tarpon. Although they can weigh close to 100 pounds, tarpon are not a danger to divers or snorkelers.

Biscayne National Park

Most visitors to the Florida Keys take Florida's Turnpike south from Miami, which feeds them onto US1 in Florida City, across the infamous '18 mile stretch' skirting the Everglades and across the Jewfish Creek bridge onto the island of Key Largo. It's easy to skip right past Biscayne National Park, which encompasses the coral reefs between Miami and Key Largo.

In addition to the outer coral reefs, the 173,000 acres of Biscayne National Park include much of Biscayne Bay and the string of undeveloped islands – including Boca Chita, Elliott and Adams Keys – between Miami and the Upper Keys. However, boats from Key Largo do not venture as far north as the Reefs in Biscayne National Park. To dive these reefs, you must come via private boat or board one of the Park's concessionaire boats at Convoy Point park visitors center. Access to Convoy Point is only a short drive from the Florida Turnpike, but once you're in the Keys you have to drive nearly back to Miami to reach the turn-off.

Live coral cover is reduced between Miami and Key Largo, but the shallow reefs and wrecks, and the vast natural resources of Biscayne National Park, are still worth the trip. For more information, visit the Biscayne National Park website at www.nps.gov/bisc.

64 WINDJAMMER

Location: *1 nautical mile (1.9km) southwest of Loggerhead Key*
Depth Range: *Surface-18ft (6m)*
Access: *Boat*
Expertise Rating: *Novice*

Also known as 'the French Wreck,' this 261ft iron-hulled sailing vessel was built in Scotland in 1875. Originally named *Killean*, then *Antonin* and also *Avanti*, she lost her rudder and ran aground on Loggerhead Reef in 1907 while carrying lumber from Pensacola to South America. All 32 crewmen were lost in the tragedy.

The maximum depth at this site is only 18ft, and parts of the wreck are exposed at low tide. The bow section has been flattened by the sea, but is still mostly intact, with the graceful bowsprit still attached. The hull is densely covered with healthy spheres of star and brain coral, one mound heaped upon the other. Schools of Bermuda chub sweep ceaselessly back and forth, winding in and out among the corals.

The ship's structure is open amidships, where it broke apart during the grounding. A section of one of the tall masts remains fastened to the vessel, but now rests flat on the sand. The two large jewfish that reside within the hull are accustomed to visitors and will tolerate a close approach.

The stern section lies on the sand a short swim from the bow. A trail of plating and broken rigging leads from one section to the other. The stern is more broken up than the bow, but still provides excellent habitat for fish, including hundreds of yellow goatfish and mangrove snappers.

The *Windjammer* is an excellent wreck for snorkelers, but photographers will probably prefer scuba. A single mooring buoy bobs between the two sections.

Snorkeling along the hull of the Windjammer

The wreck of the Windjammer is great for snorkelers and divers

Getting to the Tortugas

Following is a list of public transport options to Dry Tortugas National Park. For information on services, contact the park at ☎ 305-242-7700 or visit the website at www.nps.gov/drto.

Dry Tortugas Ferry
Yankee Freedom II
Toll free: ☎ 800-634-0939
☎ 305-294-7009
www.yankeefleet.com

Sunny Days Catamarans
Fast Cat II
Toll free: ☎ 800-236-7937
☎ 305-292-6100
www.drytortugas.com

Seaplanes of Key West
Key West International Airport
Toll free: ☎ 800-950-2359
☎ 305-294-0709
www.seaplanesofkeywest.com

Sea-Clusive Charters
17195 Kingfish Lane West
Sugarloaf Key, FL 33040
☎ 305-744-9928
www.seaclusive.com

Marine Life

Barracuda are not dangerous unless provoked

Geographically speaking, the Florida Keys are in the Atlantic, but the marine life on these reefs is remarkably similar to that found almost anywhere in the Caribbean. A complex ecosystem supports marine life here including the islands themselves, fringing mangroves, seagrass meadows, patch reef, hard bottom, sand flats and the outer reefs.

Leave this leafy fire coral alone

HAZARDOUS MARINE LIFE

Fire Coral

The most common dive injury in the Florida Keys is the burning rash caused by contact with fire coral. It can be found – and accidentally touched – nearly anywhere. Fire coral is actually not a true coral but a hydroid colony with a coral-like calcareous skeleton. It comes in two basic forms: leafy fire coral (shaped like mustard brown leaves or ribbons), and encrusting fire coral that can coat structures, ropes or even other coral, such as brain coral or sea fans.

Fire coral 'stings' by discharging small, specialized cells called nematocysts. Contact on bare skin causes a burning sensation that lasts for several minutes and may produce red welts. Do not rub the area, as you will only spread the stinging cells. Cortizone cream can reduce the inflammation and antihistamine cream is good for relieving the pain. Immersing the affected area in hot, non-scalding water may also help. Serious stings should be treated by a doctor.

Jellyfish

Stinging cells called nematocysts are responsible for the pain that jellyfish tentacles can inflict on unwary divers and snorkelers. There are three species of jellyfish to watch out for in the Florida Keys. The Portuguese man-o-war is the most dangerous. The body of this jellyfish floats on the surface, often with the tentacles trailing more than 10ft (3m) into the water. The sting from this jellyfish can be extremely painful, perhaps life-threatening to individuals with allergies.

The moon jelly is often seen along the reef line, floating in the current. They can be found at nearly any depth, but are not particularly dangerous. The tentacles can cause a mild sting or burning, similar to that produced by fire coral.

The upside-down jellyfish is found primarily in shallow water and is most common in Florida Bay. Snorkelers in this area may come into contact with the upside-down jelly while it is lying on the bottom with the tentacles facing up. The sting from this jellyfish is comparatively mild, but should be avoided.

Stings should be treated immediately with a decontaminate such as vinegar, baking soda or a paste made of meat tenderizer. People experiencing a strong reaction may need to be resuscitated and will require immediate medical attention.

Bristle Worms

Also called fire worms, bristle worms are found nearly everywhere on the reef, but are most common in reef rubble zones and seagrass beds. They are also encountered quite often on wrecks. Bristle worms have segmented bodies covered with tufts of sensory hairs that extend in fluffy looking but very sharp bristles. If you touch one, the tiny stinging bristles lodge in your skin and cause a burning sensation that may result in a red welt. Remove embedded bristles with adhesive tape, rubber cement or

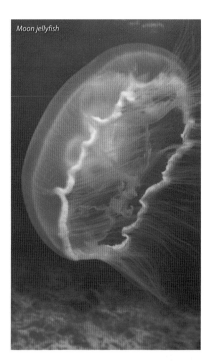
Moon jellyfish

a commercial face peel. Apply a decontaminant such as vinegar, rubbing alcohol or dilute ammonia.

Sea Urchins

Several decades ago there were thousands of long-spined sea urchins in the Florida Keys, but a Caribbean-wide blight killed most of them in 1987 and the urchins have not yet recovered. That's not so good for the reef since the urchins helped keep the algae under control, but it's good news for divers. With far fewer urchins on the reef, it's much easier to avoid their needle sharp spines.

If you do come into contact with a long-spined sea urchin, the spines will easily penetrate wet suit material and break off in your flesh. Treat minor punctures by extracting the spines and immersing the area in non-scalding hot water. More serious injuries may require medical assistance.

Steer clear of scorpionfish

Scorpionfish

These well-camouflaged fish have poisonous spines along their dorsal fins. They lie motionless on the reef or sand, hoping to surprise their prey. Since they are so difficult to see, it's possible to put your hand, foot or knee on one accidentally if you are not careful with your buoyancy.

Scorpionfish wounds can be exceptionally painful. To treat a puncture, wash the wound and immerse it in non-scalding hot water for 30 to 90 minutes. Seek medical aid if necessary.

Moray Eels

Moray eels have been a favorite with movies and television for years, where they are often portrayed as vicious killers. They do indeed have extremely sharp teeth and strong jaws. They can do a lot of damage in the blink of an eye and even a minor bite by a moray is serious. However, the truth is that you would have to go out of your way to provoke an attack by a moray eel. If you encounter an eel on the reef, keep a reasonable distance and enjoy the moment. It's always a good idea to keep

your hands and fingers away from the eel, since they could be mistaken for small fish.

In the unlikely event that you are bitten, don't try to pull your hand back quickly – the teeth slant backward and eels have an incredibly strong grip. Let the eel release your hand, then surface slowly. Treat the bite with antiseptics, anti-tetanus and antibiotics and seek medical assistance.

Barracuda

A lot of myths have circulated about barracuda, such as their propensity to attack shiny objects like dive watches or necklaces. The general experience in the Keys is that these fish, like moray eels, are not dangerous to divers and snorkelers unless directly provoked. Fishermen are much more likely to be injured while handling hooked or boated barracuda.

However, barracuda are large, quick predators with an impressive mouthful of very sharp teeth. In addition, they have a habit of closely approaching divers and snorkelers, especially when you first enter the water. Remember that thousands of people swim, snorkel

Green morays are not hazardous unless harassed

and dive in the Keys every year without being attacked by a barracuda. Keep your hands to yourself, though, because a little caution is never a bad thing.

Irrigate a barracuda bite with fresh water and treat with antiseptics, anti-tetanus and antibiotics.

Sharks

Shark encounters of any kind are actually fairly rare for divers and snorkelers in the Florida Keys. Shark attacks on divers or snorkelers are almost unheard of, and the rare instances usually involve somebody who ill-advisedly grabs a resting nurse shark by the tail.

About 25 species of shark worldwide are considered dangerous to humans. In the Florida Keys the most common sharks are nurse and reef sharks, which are not generally considered dangerous. Bull and Tiger sharks are sighted occasionally, though, and these species can be dangerous.

Sharks will generally not attack unless provoked, so don't chase, tease or feed them. Avoid spearfishing, carrying fish baits or mimicking a wounded fish, and your likelihood of being attacked will greatly diminish. Quietly face any shark that is acting aggressively and be prepared to push it away with a camera, knife or tank. If someone is bitten by a shark, stop the bleeding, reassure the patient, treat for shock and seek immediate medical assistance.

Stingrays

Identified by its diamond-shaped body and wide 'wings,' the stingray has a venomous spine at the base of its tail. This stinger is primarily a defensive weapon, used by the stingray to discourage an attacker. As with the other fish in this section, unprovoked attacks are exceedingly rare.

There are two common stingrays in the Florida Keys; the southern stingray and the yellow stingray. Southern stingrays are larger and are generally an even

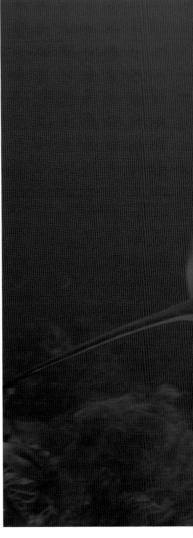

gray color. When not feeding or swimming, they tend to bury themselves partly in the sand and rest with only their eyes and gills exposed. Stepping on or attempting to handle a sleeping ray may result in a sting.

Yellow stingrays are smaller, with mottled black and yellow markings. They tend to ignore divers and will calmly

Shark encounters, like this one with a reef shark, are actually rare in the Florida Keys

continue to search for food right in front of you. Don't be fooled by their small size. If you harass a yellow stingray, you may get stung.

Though injuries from either species are uncommon, the wounds are always painful and often deep and infective. Immerse wounds in non-scalding hot water and seek medical aid.

Don't mess with the yellow stingray

Travel Facts

Sundowners restaurant in Key Largo

VISAS & DOCUMENTS

No additional visas or documents are required to visit the Florida Keys after entry into the United States.

MONEY

The US dollars is the only accepted currency. Major credit cards are accepted nearly everywhere, including rental-car agencies, hotels, restaurants, gas stations and many supermarkets. Traveler's checks are also widely accepted. ATMs are available throughout the Keys at banks, grocery stores, service stations and hotels.

The state sales tax is 6% on all purchases. In Miami the value-added tax is 6.5%, with an additional 5% tax on hotel accommodation (or 11.5% total tax on hotels).

Tipping is customary for good service. Be aware that a 15% tip may already be included in your restaurant bill. Restaurant wait staff and taxi drivers usually receive 10% to 20% of the tab. Bellhops generally expect about $1 per bag, while hotel maids should be tipped at least $1.50 a day.

COMMUNICATIONS

Telephone service – both land line and cellular – is excellent throughout the Keys. Phonecards can be purchased for long-distance calls, and many international cell phone plans allow your phone to be used in the Florida Keys. If you plan to rely on your cell phone, however, verify that you will be able to use your phone in the Keys before you leave home. Most hotels provide Internet service, usually requiring guests to provide their own laptop computers. High-speed wireless service, either in rooms or in the lobby, is becoming increasingly common. Regular postal service is available throughout the Keys. Express package services, such as FedEx and UPS are also available, although Saturday pickup and delivery is not offered.

TIME

The Florida Keys are on Eastern Standard Time and, like most of the US, observe daylight saving time. When it's noon in the Florida Keys, it's 9am in San Francisco, 5pm in London and 4am the following day in Sydney.

ELECTRICITY

Electricity throughout the US is 110–115 volts, 60 Hz AC. Most outlets accept ungrounded plugs with two parallel blades (one slightly larger than the other) or grounded plugs with two parallel blades and a rounded shaft. Though several stores sell transformers and adapters, it's best to bring your own for dive light and strobe batteries.

WEIGHTS & MEASURES

The imperial system of weights and measures is used throughout the US, although metric equivalents are sometimes supplied. Distances are in feet, yards and statute miles. Weights are in ounces, pounds and tons. Please refer to the conversion chart on the inside back cover for metric equivalents. In dive shops and aboard dive boats, distances are given in nautical miles, weights are given in pounds, air pressure is measured in pounds per square inch (psi) and depth is given in feet. Divers accustomed to the metric system should expect to perform their own conversions. In this book both imperial and metric measurements are given, except for specific references in dive site descriptions, which are given in imperial units only.

Ocean Divers: a Key Largo dive shop

The old Customs House, Key West

ACCOMMODATION

Accommodation from basic to indulgent luxury are available in the Keys. At the budget-end of the scale, campgrounds provide tent and RV sites for modest fees. You'll find single rooms, studios, suites, condos, time-shares and houses in nearly every price range. Prices vary according to the time of year, with high season running from December 30 to March 30.

Accommodation is clustered around the population centers, particularly Key Largo, Islamorada, Marathon, Big Pine Key and Key West. However, some motels, time-shares and smaller inns are available outside of these centers. Advance reservations are highly recommended, especially during the winter months and in Key West. Hotels often fill early, but travel agents can usually find you alternative accommodations if your first choice is booked.

DINING & FOOD

Dining in the Florida Keys is on par with the diving, so expect great food, lots of choices and wonderful waterfront settings. Many restaurants offer truly fresh seafood, right off the boats. There are many small, quaint places unique to the Keys along the Overseas Highway. Take a chance and stop – you'll probably be pleasantly surprised. If you feel the need for speed, all the popular fast-food chains have outlets in Key Largo, Tavernier, Marathon and Key West.

Look for large supermarkets – like Publix and Winn Dixie – in Key Largo, Tavernier, Marathon, Big Pine Key and Key West. All of these stores have extended hours. Smaller convenience stores, such as Circle K and Tom Thumb, are located every few miles along the highway. Of course, the selection of goods is much smaller than at supermarkets and the prices are generally higher, but many convenience stores are open 24 hours, seven days a week.

Don't leave without sampling at least one of the conch dishes for which the Keys are famous. Conch chowder, conch fritters and cracked conch are all made from the meat of the gastropods that lend the name 'Conchs' to Keys natives. However it's prepared, conch is delicious, if slightly chewy. Key lime pie, made with the small, tart, round limes native to the Keys is another culinary specialty that should not be missed.

Mallory Square, Key West

SHOPPING

If you're looking for large malls with national brand-name stores, plan on doing your shopping in Miami or Fort Lauderdale at the beginning or end of your trip. The Keys have a lot to offer, but the principle products are souvenirs and locally crafted gifts or jewelry. Shops selling T-shirts and inexpensive souvenirs have blossomed in Key West to service the daily flood of cruise ship passengers, but the original art galleries and fine jewelry stores are still there too.

The Keys are also a good source for water sports equipment. Several dive outlet stores and some dive shops carry large inventories at low prices. The outlets carry a variety of brands, while the product line in individual dive shops tends to be more brand selective.

GETTING THERE & AWAY

Most visitors to the Florida Keys travel via Miami or Fort Lauderdale by rental car or tour bus. Driving time from Miami International Airport to Key Largo is about an hour and a half. Marathon is about 2½ hours from Miami, while Key West is 3½ to four hours from Miami.

To reach the Keys from Miami, get on Florida's Turnpike Extension headed south. At Florida City the turnpike ends, funneling you onto US1 South. Immediately after Florida City you have a choice: take Card Sound Rd or continue south on US1. The Card Sound route is slightly longer and has a toll bridge, but there's also less traffic. US1 is shorter, but includes the dreaded '18-mile stretch,' which can back up with slow traffic. Either way you'll end up on Key Largo.

Sunset celebration, Mallory Square in Key West

The Overseas Highway at Whale Harbor and Holiday Isle

There are also direct flights to Key West International Airport, with connections from Orlando, Fort Myers, Naples, Fort Lauderdale or Miami. Limited connections are also available to Marathon. Rental cars are available in Key Largo, Marathon and Key West.

GETTING AROUND

Rental cars are the most popular mode of transportation among visitors to the Keys. The Overseas Highway is an easy drive and, except in Key West, free parking is readily available. A car can be a necessity for divers, since many dive shops and boats are not based at the hotels.

Taxis operate throughout the Keys, providing local service as well as transportation to and from Miami. Arrangements should be made in advance for transportation to and from the Miami and Fort Lauderdale airports. Check the yellow pages for taxi and limousine listings.

A bike path runs intermittently alongside the Overseas Highway. It is continuous through Key Largo, but terminates just north of Tavernier, reappearing at intervals between Tavernier and Key West. Use caution on the bike path as motorists

Shuttle Services

Several shuttle services provide transportation between the Keys and Miami International Airport, including:
The Airporter
☎ 305-451-0585
Keys Shuttle
☎ 305-289-9997
Emerald Transportation
☎ 305-852-1468
Flamingo Benz
☎ 305-853-3001
Just Jeeps of the Keys
☎ 305-367-1070
Islamorada Taxi
☎ 305-664-4100
Sunset Taxi
☎ 305-872-4233

Greyhound Bus Lines runs a regular service between Miami and Key West ☎ 800-410-5397.

are often oblivious to bicycles and fail to yield the right of way. Bike helmets are not required by Florida law, but wearing one is highly recommended. Key West is reasonably bike-friendly, particularly

if you stay on designated bike paths. Rental bikes are available in Key Largo, Marathon and Key West, with models ranging from single-speed beach cruisers to sophisticated mountain bikes.

Rental mopeds are also popular in Key West, where parking can be at a premium. Ride cautiously – other motorists may not see you.

Rental boats are available throughout the Keys, but are recommended for experienced boaters only. Navigation can be tricky, and running aground will be expensive because you'll be fined for damage to the coral or seagrass as well as the boat. If you want to rent a boat, but don't feel confident about navigating in the Keys, go out once or twice with a dive operator first to get a feel for the area. When you do take a boat out, be sure you have a large-scale chart and know how to read it.

The Overseas Highway (US1) is the only road from Key Largo to Key West. Directions to places along the highway are given by specifying the mile marker (MM) and often which side of the road, as in MM 49.2 oceanside, or MM 99 bayside. In addition to these simple directions, you may hear people refer to the Upper, Middle and Lower Keys. These are general divisions; unofficial but useful when talking about what goes on where. In this book, the Upper Keys include islands from Key Largo to Long Key (MM 107 to MM 66), the Middle Keys from the Long Key Viaduct to Vaca Key (MM 65 to MM 47), and the Lower Keys from the Seven Mile Bridge to Key West (MM 46 to MM 0), although locals often refer to Key West (MM 12 to MM 0) as a separate entity.

Most visitors to the Keys arrive initially in Miami

Listings

UPPER KEYS

Amoray Dive Resort
104250 Overseas Hwy
Key Largo, FL 33037
☎ 800-426-6729, 800-4-AMORAY,
305-451-3595
www.amoray.com

Admiral Dive Center
MM 98.7 Overseas Hwy
Key Largo, FL 33037
☎ 800-346-DIVE,
305-451-1114
www.admiralcenter.com

Aqua-Nut Divers
104220 Overseas Hwy
Key Largo, FL 33037
☎ 800-226-0415, 305-451-1622
www.aqua-nuts.com

Atlantis Dive Center
51 Garden Cove Drive
Key Largo, FL 33037
☎ 305-451-1325
www.pennekamp.com/atlantis

Blue Water Divers
99701 Overseas Hwy
Key Largo, FL 33037
☎ 888-953-9600, 305-453-9600
www.bluewaterdiver.net

Caribbean Watersports
Sheraton Beach Resort
97000 Overseas Hwy
Key Largo, FL 33037
☎ 800-223-6728, 305-852-4707
www.caribbeanwatersports.com

Conch Republic Divers
90800 Overseas Hwy
Tavernier, FL 33070
☎ 800-274-DIVE, 305-852-1655
www.conchrepublicdivers.com

Dive In
PO Box 2255
Key Largo, FL 33037
☎ 877-453-6169, 305-852-1919
www.diveinflkeys.com

Divers City USA
90511 Overseas Hwy
Tavernier, FL 33070
☎ 800-649-4659, 305-852-0430
www.diverscityusa.com

Florida Keys Dive Center
PO Box 391
Tavernier, FL 33070
☎ 800-433-8946,
305-852-4599
www.floridakeysdivectr.com

Garden Cove Divers
21 Garden Cove Drive
MM 106.2
Key Largo, FL 33037
☎ 305-395-9555
www.gardencovedivers.com

Horizon Divers
100 Ocean Drive – Bldg 1
Key Largo, FL 33037
☎ 800-984-DIVE, 305-453-3535
www.horizondivers.com

HMS Minnow
PO Box 1104
Key Largo, FL 33037
☎ 800-366-9301,
305-451-7834
www.hmsminnow.com

Holiday Isle Dive Shop
Mile Marker 84.5
Islamorada, FL 33036
☎ 800-327-7070 x644,
305-664-DIVE
www.diveholidayisle.com

Island Ventures
PO Box 306
MM 103.9 Overseas Hwy
Key Largo, FL 33037
☎ 866-293-5006, 305-451-4957
www.islandventure.com

Island Reef Diver
3 Seagate Blv, Key Largo, FL 33037
☎ 305-453-9456
www.islandreefdiver.com

It's A Dive
103800 Overseas Hwy
Key Largo, FL 33037
☎ 800-809-9881, 305-453-9881
www.itsadive.com

John Pennekamp State Park Concession
PO Box 1560
102601 Overseas Hwy
Key Largo, FL 33037
☎ 877-LETS DIVE, 305-451-1621
www.pennekamppark.com

Jules Undersea Lodge
51 Shoreland Drive
Key Largo, FL 33037
☎ 305-451-2353
www.jul.com

Keys Diver Snorkel Tours
99696 Overseas Hwy
Key Largo, FL 33037
☎ 888-289-2402, 305-451-1177
www.keysdiver.com

Ocean Divers
522 Caribbean Drive
Key Largo, FL 33037
☎ 800-451-1113, 305-451-1113
www.oceandivers.com

Ocean Quest Dive Center, Inc.
MM 85.5 Overseas Hwy
Islamorada, FL 33036
☎ 800-356-8798, 305-664-4401
www.oceanquestdivecenter.com

Pleasure Diver
MM 100 Overseas Hwy
Key Largo, FL 33037
☎ 800-294-7939, 305-853-5384
www.pleasurediver.com

Quicksilver Catamaran Snorkel and Sail
PO Box 659
Key Largo, FL 33037
☎ 800-347-9972, 305-451-0105
www.quicksilversnorkel.com

Quiescence Diving Services
PO Box 1570 Mile Marker 103.5
Key Largo, FL 33037
☎ 305-451-2440
www.keylargodiving.com
www.quiescence.com

Rainbow Reef Dive Center
99725 and 85500 Overseas Hwy
Islamorada, FL 33036
☎ 800-457-4354, 305-664-4600
www.rainbowreef.us

Scuba-Do Charters
522 Caribbean Drive
Key Largo, FL 33037
☎ 800-516-0110, 305-451-3446
www.scuba-do.com

Sea Dwellers Dive Center
99850 Overseas Hwy
Key Largo, FL 33037
☎ 800-451-3640, 305-451-3640
www.sea-dwellers.com

Silent World Dive Center
103200 Overseas Hwy
Key Largo, FL 33037
☎ 800-966-3483, 305-451-3252
www.silentworldkeylargo.com

Snorkeling by Sundiver
PO Box 963 102840 Overseas Hwy
Key Largo, FL 33037
☎ 800-654-7369, 305-451-2220
www.snorkelingisfun.com

Stephen Frink Photographic
PO Box 2720
MM 102.5 Overseas Hwy
Key Largo, FL 33037
☎ 800-451-3737, 305-451-3737
www.stephenfrink.com

Tavernier Dive Center
PO Box 465
88005 Old Hwy
Islamorada, FL 33036
☎ 800-787-9797, 305-852-4007
www.tavernierdivecenter.com

Upper Keys Dive and Sport Center
90701 Old Hwy, Tavernier, FL 33070
☎ 800-537-3253, 305-852-8799
www.tropicvistadiveresort.com/upper-keysdive.htm

World Down Under Water Sports
80001 Overseas Hwy
Upper Matacumbe, FL 33036
☎ 800-834-9312, 305-664-9312
www.worlddownunder.net

MIDDLE KEYS

Abyss Dive Center
13175 Overseas Hwy
Marathon, FL 33050
☎ 800-457-0134, 305-743-2126
www.abyssdive.com

Aquatic Adventure
PO Box 510378
Key Colony Beach, FL 33051
☎ 305-743-2421

Capt. Hook's Dive Center
11833 Overseas Hwy
Marathon, FL 33050
☎ 800-278-4665, 305-743-2444
www.captainhooks.com

Hall's Diving Center
1994 Overseas Hwy
Marathon, FL 33050
☎ 800-331-4255, 305-743-5929
www.hallsdiving.com

Middle Keys Scuba Center
11511 Overseas Hwy
Marathon, FL 33050
☎ 305-743-2902
www.divingdiscovery.com

Reef Runner
PO Box 1056
Marathon, FL 33050
☎ 800-332-8899, 305-289-9808
www.floridadivecharter.com

Sombrero Reef Explorers, Inc.
19 Sombrero Blvd
Marathon, FL 33050
☎ 305-743-0536
www.sombreroreef.com

LOWER KEYS

Innerspace Dive Center
PO Box 430651
Mile Marker 29.5
Big Pine Key, FL 33043
☎ 800-538-2896,
305-872-2319
www.diverinnerspace.com

Looe Key Reef Resort
PO Box 509
Mile Marker 27.5
Ramrod Key, FL 33042
☎ 800-LOOE-KEY,
305-872-2215
www.diveflakeys.com

Paradise Divers
38801 Overseas Hwy
Mile Marker 39
Big Pine Key, FL 33043
☎ 305-872-1114
www.paradivers.com

Strike Zone Charters, Inc.
29675 Overseas Hwy
Mile Marker 29.5
Big Pine Key, FL 33043
☎ 800-654-9560,
305-872-9863
www.strikezonecharter.com

Underseas, Inc.
PO Box 319 Mile Marker 30.5
Big Pine Key, FL 33043
☎ 800-446-5663, 305-872-2700
www.seefloridaonline.com

KEY WEST

Bonsai Diving
1075 Duval Street
Key West, FL 33040
☎ 305-294-2921, 305-296-6301
www.bonsaidiving.com

Dive Key West
3128 North Roosevelt Blvd
Key West, FL 33040
☎ 800-426-0707, 305-296-3823
www.divekeywest.com

Key West Diving Society
951 Caroline St
Key West, FL 33040
☎ 866-KW-DIVER, 305-292-3221
www.keywestdivingsociety.com

Lost Reef Adventures, Inc.
261 Margaret Street
Key West, FL 33040
☎ 800-952-2749, 305-296-9737
www.lostreefadventures.com

Sea Breeze Reef Raiders
617 Front St
Key West, FL 33040
☎ 800-370-7745, 305-292-7745
www.keywestscubadive.com

Southpoint Divers
500 Truman Ave
Key West, FL 33040
☎ 800-891-DIVE, 305-292-9778
www.southpointdivers.com

Subtropic Dive Center
1605 North Roosevelt Blvd
Key West, FL 33040
☎ 800-853-DIVE, 305-296-9914
www.subtropic.com

FORT JEFFERSON & THE DRY TORTUGAS

Dry Tortugas Ferry
Yankee Freedom II
☎ 800-634-0939, 305-294-7009
www.yankeefleet.com

Seaplanes of Key West
Key West International Airport
☎ 800-950-2359, 305-294-0709
www.seaplanesofkeywest.com

Sunny Days Catamarans
Fast Cat II
☎ 800-236-7937, 305-292-6100
www.drytortugas.com

Sea-Clusive Charters
17195 Kingfish Lane West
Sugarloaf Key, FL 33040
☎ 305-744-9928
www.seaclusive.com

Index

THIS IS NOT
THE END

www.lonelyplanet.com